TRADE-OFFS

TRADE-OFFS

An Introduction to Economic Reasoning and Social Issues

HAROLD WINTER

THE UNIVERSITY OF CHICAGO PRESS

Chicago and London

HAROLD WINTER is associate professor of economics at Ohio University.

The University of Chicago Press, Chicago 60637
The University of Chicago Press, Ltd., London
© 2005 by The University of Chicago
All rights reserved. Published 2005
Printed in the United States of America

14 13 12 11 10 09 08 07 06 05   1 2 3 4 5

ISBN: 0-226-90224-2 (cloth)
ISBN: 0-226-90225-0 (paper)

Library of Congress Cataloging-in-Publication Data

Winter, Harold, 1960–
    Trade-offs : an introduction to economic reasoning and social issues / Harold Winter.
    p. cm.
    Includes bibliographical references and index.
    ISBN 0-226-90224-2 (cloth : alk. paper) — ISBN 0-226-90225-0 (pbk. : alk. paper)
    1. Economics. 2. Reasoning. 3. Public policy. 4. Social policy. 5. Ethics. I. Title.
    HB171.W764 2005
    330′.01′156—dc22

                                                            2004016360

To my parents for creating a monster and to Jenn for living with one.

Contents

Preface: Welcome to My World   ix
Acknowledgments   xiii

1   Approaching Social Issues   1
2   A Valuable Life (to Some Extent)   9
3   Do You Want to Trade?   21
4   What's Yours Is Mine   33
5   Smoke If You Got 'Em   49
6   Stop Bothering Me   67
7   Behave Yourself   87
8   Warning: Beware of Products   101
9   There Are No Solutions   117

Index   125

Preface: Welcome to My World

HELLO. My name is Harold Winter and I am a professor of economics at Ohio University. My main field of interest is economics of law, and my job description involves basically two things—teaching and research. But as a bonus, I often get the opportunity to use economic reasoning to frighten people.

For example, a couple of years ago my mother was visiting me. I have a nice relationship with my mother, but we don't often talk about social issues. One night, however, she asked me what I had talked about in class that day. Usually I would have little to say about what I teach, especially when I am teaching formal economic theory courses. But that day was special: I was doing an independent reading course with a very bright student. We were reading a book about the American health care system written by an intense free-market-oriented legal scholar. In one of the chapters we discussed that day, the author argued that it may be sensible social policy to allow overworked emergency rooms to refuse care to patients who couldn't pay or who didn't have insurance. As I told my mother about this, I went into "professor mode" and ranted on for about ten minutes, showing her my passion for economic reasoning. When I was finished, she had a scared look in her eyes and then simply said, "You're a monster!"

Being called a monster by my mother didn't really bother me, but I started thinking about how completely alien economic reasoning is to some people. I think what surprises many people about economics is that it can be applied to an extremely broad range of issues. Most people expect economists to talk about unemployment, inflation, or the budget deficit, but not about organ transplants, cigarette addiction, or secondhand smoke. But economists can place just about any issue into an economic context, sometimes even to the surprise of other economists.

When I was a graduate student in Rochester, New York, I was once in a professor's office when his phone rang. From his end of the conversation, all I heard him say was: "I'll get there as soon as I can." After he hung up the phone he told me he had to leave immediately to be a consultant for a hospital in Boston. I jokingly asked him if they needed his permission to perform an operation. He said that was exactly what they needed. And he wasn't kidding! The doctors were deciding between some different procedures, and they wanted his opinion on the cost-effectiveness of each one. Can you imagine lying on an operating table and the surgeon tells you not to worry because the economist is on his way?

When using economic reasoning to approach social issues, the concepts of right and wrong can become very murky. I have always found this comforting. When I was young, whenever my parents told me I was wrong about something, I always responded by saying "from whose point of view?" Although that response rarely impressed my parents, I always maintained that the concepts of right and wrong were often a matter of perspective. As I became more exposed to economic reasoning, I came to realize that there is a whole academic discipline that shares this view. Instead of focusing on what is right or wrong, economists focus on costs and benefits.

Cost-benefit analysis allows economists to *detach* themselves not only from their personal views, but also from favoring one side or the other of whatever social issue is at hand. What this entails will be made clear as I discuss specific issues throughout this book, such as product safety, copyright protection, and secondhand smoke. I have my own personal opinions about some of these issues, but it is my professional opinion I intend to relate to you. The mantra I teach my students is this: *if you are on one side of an issue, you are on the wrong side*. I don't expect my students to accept this mantra in their personal lives, but I *require* them to accept it in my class.

In this book, I will be focusing primarily on theoretical issues as opposed to empirical issues or policy solutions. I am going to use many abstract and hypothetical situations to introduce you to economic reasoning. I am not going to present economic reasoning as a cure-all for real-world problems. My goal is far more modest. I simply want to present you with a unique way of thinking about social issues, one that allows you to sidestep some of the moral, ethical, or legal arguments that often are used in public policy debate. Keep in mind that in no way am I claiming that these other concerns are unimportant, and I recognize that they are generally at the forefront of public policy debate. I only want to present economic reasoning as *a* way of thinking about social issues, not *the* way of thinking about them. I do believe, however, that economic reasoning is an important and valid way of thinking about social issues.

Many of the topics I will discuss have been analyzed in tremendous detail by many types of scholars. My goal is to introduce you to basic economic reasoning, and not to present you with a thorough discussion of all of these details. Furthermore, there are numerous issues I will not cover at all in an attempt to keep my presentation as concise as possible. If you are reading this book as a supplemental text in some policy course, I am sure you will appreciate my brevity. I will provide several references at the end of each chapter for the interested reader to further pursue the topics I discuss, and many others, in greater detail.

I wrote this book in conjunction with preparing a course in health economics, thus many of the issues I will discuss here are health related. Because the course was interdisciplinary in nature, my goal was to make the material accessible to students who had little or no background in economics. The material was presented with no graphs, no math, few statistics, and a few numerical examples when needed for ease of exposition. I will continue with that approach throughout this book.

Throughout the years, I have had many discussions of social issues with friends, colleagues, students, and family members. I will relate some of these conversations to you, but usually keep the names of the other parties involved anonymous. In case my memory is faulty, I apologize to those other parties for possible misrepresentations of their views and comments. I assure you that any misrepresentation was done accidentally, unless it was done to be entertaining.

NOTES

The book on the American health care system is by Richard Epstein, *Mortal Peril: Our Inalienable Right to Health Care?* (Reading, MA: Addison-Wesley Publishing Co., 1997).

Acknowledgments

MY FIRST debt of gratitude goes to Alex Schwartz, senior editor at the University of Chicago Press. Throughout our correspondence, Alex's interest in this project and the encouragement he gave me was without bounds. I have never seen so much energy come from one person. I'm just glad he uses his powers for good instead of evil. I also got to work closely with Catherine Beebe and Mara Naselli. Catherine had the magic touch in picking reviewers, and Mara made my words sound like they were written by someone who knows how to write. Both demonstrated a phenomenal amount of enthusiasm for this project. I also appreciate their patience in dealing with the thousands of questions I asked along the way. And to Peter Cavagnaro and everyone else at the Press who has contributed to the publication of this book, thanks for making this the most enjoyable publishing experience I have ever had.

As a student, I had the good fortune to have two academic mentors. Eric Hanushek, my graduate mentor and the nicest economist in the world, made important comments on an early version of this book that significantly affected the way I decided to write it. Gwill Allen, my undergraduate mentor who currently is an anticompetitive watchdog for the Canadian government, also provided helpful comments. These guys are economists' economists. Thanks for all your help over the years.

I have also had the good fortune to be the mentor of several excellent students. Three in particular, Jeff Baird, Ryan Richey, and Michael Taylor have engaged me in many challenging discussions about economics and public policy. Thanks for keeping me sharp. I also want to thank the students who have taken my health economics course for their patience in watching me develop a new course. It was a great teaching experience for me. Thanks to Tiffany Margrave for assisting me in collecting readings for the course.

I also benefited from many conversations and comments from my colleagues at Ohio University. Early on in the writing process, I had many conversations about the material in this book over chicken wings with Donald Lacombe. Julia Paxton read the first draft of the book and let me know I was on the right track. Ariaster Chimeli, Charlene Kalenkoski, David Klingaman, and Rosemary Rossiter all read the manuscript and made helpful comments. Also, I thank Roy Boyd for giving me plenty of time to prepare the health economics course.

I owe a special debt of gratitude to William Neilson, my good friend and coauthor. Bill has taught me more about doing research than anyone else I know. His critical reading of the manuscript allowed me to make substantial improvements. And after all the reviews for this book were in, he asked me if his was the harshest. Yes it was, and I appreciate it.

I would also like to thank the anonymous reviewers for their thoughtful comments. Other reviewers who were not anonymous, Edward Foster, Joni Hersch, and Kate Wahl, are also greatly thanked.

I also want to thank my family for their never-ending support. My parents provided me with several stories for this book, my sister collected Canadian cigarette packages for me to use in show and tell in my classes, and my brother and his family listened to my rants on more than one occasion.

Finally, I want to thank Jenn for making me happy.

1　*Approaching Social Issues*

IN ANALYZING social issues, I was trained as an economist not to make moral judgments about right and wrong, but to try to identify the trade-offs—that is, the costs and benefits—of whatever issue is at hand. I have seen many of my students struggle with this approach, not just in terms of performing well on their exams, but in accepting it as a legitimate way to think about public policy. To introduce them to the economic way of thinking, I present an approach to resolving social issues that has three steps:

Step 1: Identify the theoretical trade-offs of the issue in question. This is the costs and benefits step, a concept that is very familiar to every economist. Regardless of the issue, there are always trade-offs to consider. Furthermore, for any policy solution proposed, there will be those in favor of it as well as those against it. If everyone could agree on the resolution of a social issue, it wouldn't be much of an issue in the first place. Economists have a way of identifying costs and benefits that few others would ever consider, largely due to our ability to detach ourselves from many of the personal concerns that can complicate policy analysis. We can argue in favor of drug abuse, theft, and even death. We can argue against safer products and pollution control. In sum, economists are a lot of fun to talk to at parties.

Step 2: If possible, empirically measure the trade-offs to determine if the costs outweigh the benefits, or vice versa. If you are interested in proposing a policy solution, it helps to have some idea of the relative magnitude of the trade-offs you identified in step 1. To justify your solution, it generally will be useful to argue that the benefits of your solution outweigh the costs. How you want to measure the trade-offs is an important issue. You may just have a sincere gut feeling about the value of your solution, or you may want to pull out the serious statistical tools to support your claim. Either way, step 2 can be a difficult stage, for several reasons.

First, empirical analysis requires data, which can come from several sources such as surveys, observable market information, or controlled experiments. Unfortunately, data collection is often difficult to do and as a result, data are often measured inaccurately. Second, the real world is a big and messy place to study. A lot of data that ideally would be needed to accurately measure trade-offs simply may not be available. Third, there are many different statistical methods that can be used to measure the same trade-offs. Advances in computer technology and statistical software have made it possible for almost anyone with a computer to do sophisticated empirical work, so you often get to see many different approaches to the same problem. Finally, not only can the empirical approaches differ in statistical techniques, but also in empirical design. What data are most relevant? If there are alternative ways to measure the same variable, which measure should be used?

Fortunately, there are procedures that deal with many of these problems, and the best empirical work deals openly with these shortcomings. What I believe is most important for empirical work is to allow others to be able to verify the integrity of your data, and to be able to replicate your results. But this may not always be possible if there are proprietary rights that make the sharing of data impossible. Still, being able to examine the robustness of the results of any particular study is important in determining the value of that study.

It is often the case that you can have a group of economists who are in complete agreement over step 1, but in complete disagreement over step 2. I should point out, however, that disagreement over step 2 in no way diminishes the value of economic reasoning. There are legitimate and passionate disagreements in how to measure trade-offs, but this simply is an unavoidable consequence of the nature of empirical work. Any academic discipline that attempts to apply empirical analysis to policy issues will have to confront these same problems.

Step 3: Recommend (or implement) social policy based on the first two steps. This may be the most exciting step if you are passionate about public policy. While there are some economists who are in a position to actually implement social policy, the bulk of public policy economic research is meant to imply, or recommend, policy solutions. Many economists keep their research largely to themselves and to a small group of scholars who are interested in the same issues. But some economists step out into the public arena and make their positions clear. The fun begins not only when other economists are right out there bumping heads with them, but when scholars and analysts from all walks of life are also thrown into the mix. Step 3 is where you get to flex your muscles and find out if anyone who is in a position to make policy decisions actually cares about what you have to say. This step is definitely the loudest of the three steps.

Taken together, I believe that these three steps present a reasonably coherent approach to public policy analysis: identify trade-offs, measure trade-offs, and recommend policy. These steps on their own, however, are still incomplete. They have no policy relevance until a policy *objective* can be identified.

OBJECTIVELY SPEAKING

As outlined above, many of the academic debates over public policy occur due to the difficulties associated with step 2, the empirical measurement of trade-offs. But there are also difficulties in pursuing the other two steps. It is one thing to say that we are going to identify trade-offs, but it is another thing to say exactly *which* trade-offs we are going to identify. In a perfect world, it would be nice to identify every conceivable cost and benefit associated with a policy solution, no matter how far-reaching the trade-offs may run. In practice, however, and even in theory, only the most relevant trade-offs are usually considered.

And this, in turn, often depends on what policy objective is being considered.

If you are going to recommend or implement public policy, you need to have a policy objective. For example, let's assume that we *can* accurately and unambiguously identify and measure costs and benefits. This would appear to make policy analysis an easy task. Propose a policy solution. If the benefits of the solution outweigh the costs, adopt the solution. If not, abandon the solution. If there is more than one solution, find the one that has the greatest spread between benefits and costs. This is a common economic approach to public policy as economists are often solely concerned with maximizing the spread between social benefits and social costs, or what is often referred to as *social welfare* (or social *wealth*) maximization.

If our policy goal is to maximize social welfare, we want to try to identify trade-offs that affect social welfare. For example, assume a new workplace safety regulation is being enforced in which a specific safety feature must be installed. A benefit of the regulation is that it may reduce worker injury or death. A cost of the regulation involves the resources that must be used to physically install and maintain the safety feature. Whatever trade-offs are identified, we can then move on to the next step and measure them.

In measuring trade-offs, it is common for economists to place a monetary value on all of the relevant costs and benefits. For example, the installation of the safety feature will involve direct costs that are likely already measured in dollars. But there may be less direct costs, such as the value of lost production if the plant must be closed down while the feature is being installed, or if workers have to spend time in training sessions. Dollar equivalents can also be established for these costs. On the benefits side, a dollar value equivalent can be established for the value of lives saved or injuries avoided. Although this may seem coarse, all of the trade-offs we identify must be measured in the same units, such as dollars, to allow for a direct comparison of the costs and benefits of the safety feature. Thus, social welfare is often measured in dollars.

Even if there is agreement on the broad objective of maximizing social welfare, policy objectives may differ due to differences in the definition of social welfare. A good example of this problem can be found in the economic analysis of crime. To deter crime, we must use resources for the apprehension, conviction, and punishment of criminals. These costs are offset by the benefits in crime reduction. But should the benefits that accrue to individuals who commit crime be added to social welfare? If yes, this may suggest that fewer resources can be used to deter crime because crime itself has offsetting benefits. If no, crime is more costly to society and more resources may be needed for deterrence. Notice, however, that it is a *fact* that a criminal reaps a benefit from committing a crime (or why commit the crime?), yet it is an *opinion* as to whether or not that benefit should be counted as social welfare. Policy objectives and definitions of social welfare are *subjectively* determined. This accounts for why social issue debates are often extremely contentious.

What, then, should be counted as social welfare? Throughout this book, what counts as social welfare will depend on the specific topic of interest, whether it is safety regulation, product liability, secondhand smoke, or copyright protection. Economists tend toward inclusiveness in defining social welfare. That is, they tend to be concerned about identifying the existence of costs and benefits, and not concerned about who reaps the benefits or incurs the costs. In other words, a dollar is a dollar, regardless of who gets the dollar. But this leads to another problem. Even if we can agree on all the trade-offs that should be included in social welfare, we may disagree on the appropriate social policy goal. For example, instead of only being concerned with welfare maximization (*efficiency*), we may also want to be concerned with how that wealth is distributed (*equity*).

Distribution of wealth issues can be very difficult to deal with. The concept of fairness tends to be open-ended. For example, what if you and I are trying to split $1000? If I suggest that we each get $500, I wouldn't be surprised if you considered that to be a fair split. But what if I am rich and you are poor? Maybe, then, to remedy that inequity you should get $750 while I get only $250. Wouldn't that be fair? But then again, if I am rich and you are poor, $250 may be as valuable to you as $750 would be to me. After all, we may want to consider how each dollar increases our levels of happiness *on the margin*. If a rich person is not likely to value one extra dollar as much as a poor person would, to be fair we may want the rich person to get more. The important point with this exercise is that one can rationalize *any* split of the $1000.

In all, proposing policy solutions can lead to endless debate. Even if there is agreement on the objective of social welfare maximization, there may be disagreement as to what should be included in the definition of social welfare. And even if there is agreement over the definition, there may be disagreement over the appropriate goals of social policy. How, then, are we to proceed with the three step approach to resolving social issues?

MY GAME PLAN

In this book, I am going to focus primarily on step 1. Identifying trade-offs is what I personally am most interested in doing as an economist, and I enjoy thinking abstractly about social issues. Furthermore, step 1 is the least contentious step among economists as there is generally a strong agreement over the identification of costs and benefits. Finally, step 1 is where economic policy analysis begins.

Although I will discuss several empirical studies throughout this book, step 2 will not be emphasized. I prefer to focus on the least contentious aspects of economic analysis. More to the point, the important debates over empirical work do not really involve the opposing results of the studies. Instead, the debates focus primarily on choice of data and statistical techniques. If you have some basic background in statistical economics (what economists refer to as *econometrics*), discussing how empirical studies differ can be an important and fascinating exercise. I'm going to assume, however, that the typical reader of this book does not have such a background. If you do have further interest in empirical research, I will provide you with several references at the end of each chapter.

As for step 3, one thing I certainly will not do is to present my recommendations for policy solutions. What I personally think about public policy issues has absolutely no bearing on understanding basic economic reasoning. What I will do, however, is often consider the goal of social welfare maximization (that is, maximizing the spread between social benefits and social costs) as my policy objective. How social welfare is defined will depend on the specific issue at hand, and this will become clearer in the chapters to come. I will not, however, be concerned with distributive issues.

I do want to make it clear that in no way I am arguing that the objective of social welfare maximization is what policy decision makers actually *do* care about. The economics field of *public choice* addresses the issue of what policy makers do care about, and if you have further interest in that topic, I recommend that you find out more about that field. I am also not going to claim that social welfare maximization is the objective that policy makers *should* care about. There are many legitimate social policy goals, and what policy makers should care about is a matter of opinion.

My main reason for focusing on a specific economic objective is that it will allow me to place the trade-offs I identify into a policy context, and I believe that this will facilitate my presentation of economic reasoning. Try to think of identifying trade-offs in the context of social welfare maximization as an abstract exercise, designed to teach you how to think like an economist, not to teach you how to resolve complex real world social issues. Although the ultimate goal of policy analysis is to answer questions about how to resolve these issues, I want to focus on the first step toward that goal—*raising* the appropriate questions about trade-offs. No matter how you decide to measure trade-offs, or how you decide to consider trade-offs in any social policy objective context, *trade-offs always exist*. No amount of disagreement about public policy issues can ever change that fact.

NOTES

If you want to learn more about applying statistical techniques to economics, there is a an excellent source by Peter Kennedy, *A Guide to Econometrics*, 5th ed. (Cambridge, MA: MIT Press, 2003).

The use of efficiency and equity criteria in identifying social policy objectives is currently a much-discussed topic largely due to the recent book by Louis Kaplow and Steven Shavell,

Fairness versus Welfare (Cambridge, MA: Harvard University Press, 2002). Also, see the following book reviews: Daniel A. Farber, "What (If Anything) Can Economics Say About Equity," *Michigan Law Review* 101 (2003): 1791–1823; David Dolinko, "The Perils of Welfare Economics," *Northwestern University Law Review* 97 (2002): 351–93; Ward Farnsworth, "The Taste for Fairness," *Columbia Law Review* 102 (2002): 1992–2026; and Jules L. Coleman, "The Grounds of Welfare," *Yale Law Journal* 112 (2003): 1511–37.

2 A Valuable Life (to Some Extent)

I **ATTENDED** a dinner party several years ago that was also attended by a new professor in the health administration department. Professors who are fresh out of graduate school are often wildly enthusiastic about intellectual discussions, and she was no exception. As we sat down to dinner, all of a sudden she began to question me about economic studies that attempt to place a dollar value on human life. She had seen some of these studies in graduate school, and was uncomfortable with the idea of equating a person's life with a finite dollar amount. She felt that a human life can only be infinitely valued, and she used the words *immoral* and *repulsive* to describe the studies that contradicted her view.

In response, I told her that I could easily convince her that she herself did not place an infinite value on her own life. She was confident that I couldn't convince her of any such thing, but she allowed me the opportunity to try. First, I asked her if she had driven to the dinner party that night. She said yes. I then asked her if she believed it was possible, even just slightly possible, for her to have been killed in an accident on her way to the party. Again, she said yes. Finally, I asked her why she would take even the slightest risk of losing her infinitely-valued life, especially just to attend a dinner party. She thought about it for a minute, and then conceded that I had a valid point. I hope she didn't think I meant that she should never leave her house again!

My point was that what some economists do explicitly, virtually every individual does implicitly—they place a finite value on human life. Economists, as well as other researchers, routinely use a *statistical value of life estimate* in policy analysis to measure trade-offs. This is the value of life in a cost-benefit analysis sense: the dollar cost of improved safety must be compared to the dollar benefit of improved safety. If the benefit is measured in lives saved, a dollar value of life is important to determine. This fact will be made painfully clear in the following section.

THE FORD PINTO

The Ford Pinto case represents a tragic example of the application of value of life estimates in a cost-benefit framework. On an Indiana highway in 1978, three girls between the ages of sixteen and eighteen were hit from behind while driving a Ford Pinto. The Pinto caught on fire, exploded, killed two of the girls immediately, and the other died a short time later from severe burns.

In an unprecedented move, the district attorney brought criminal charges of reckless homicide against Ford. Apparently, had Ford made an $11 modification in the design of the Pinto, the deaths of the girls may have been avoided. Furthermore, Ford was well aware of this because their engineers had undertaken a cost-benefit analysis in which they had assigned a dollar value to the potential loss of human life in the event of just such an accident. The conclusion of the analysis was that it was more cost effective for Ford to pay damages to the families of accident victims than it was to make the modification. Thus, concluded the prosecuting attorney, Ford had arrogantly, and criminally, traded lives for dollars.

Exactly what did the Ford engineers do? To begin with, they calculated the cost of an $11 modification for the total number of Pintos on the road. This yielded an amount of approximately $138 million. Next, they determined how many individuals would probably be killed or injured in a rear-end Pinto collision, and using average liability amounts from wrongful death and injury litigation, they calculated their legal liability of not using the modification. Using a liability amount of $200,000 for each person killed, and another amount of $67,000 for each person injured, they totaled their overall liability at approximately $50 million.

(This also included a small amount for the cost of the damaged Pintos.) Because the former figure dwarfed the latter one, Ford concluded that it would be cost effective *not* to use the modification but rather to pay civil liability when required to do so.

Even if you accept the cost-benefit analysis and the numbers Ford used, a common response about the Pinto case is "What was Ford thinking?" Let's face it. Why not just put the $11 modification in the car and charge $11 more for a Pinto? Lives would be saved, and how could $11 more in the price of a Pinto really affect anyone? This is a very persuasive argument, but only if you do not delve a bit deeper into the problem.

Have you ever considered how many thousands of decisions must go into something as complicated as product design for an automobile? There are so many margins for an automobile manufacturer to consider, many of which involve safety considerations. Any single improvement in safety may cost just a few dollars, but if there are hundreds of potential safety modifications to consider, the improvements in safety may cost thousands of dollars. And even if government regulations dictate minimum standards for a number of safety features, these decisions still have to be made by some agency. How, then, are these decisions to be made? What criteria should be used? If a safety feature involves lives saved, how are we to value those lives saved? As mentioned earlier, it is senseless to place an infinite value on human life. In that extreme case, the only really sound safety feature for an automobile would be not to produce any at all.

So, what did Ford do wrong? Did they make a sound business decision? Quite possibly, yes. But a sound business decision from Ford's perspective may not be a sound business decision from society's perspective. Proper cost-benefit analysis doesn't only require using a value of life estimate, it requires using the appropriate one. But what is meant by *appropriate?*

HOW VALUABLE IS A LIFE?

In a *wrongful death* case, part of the issue that must be determined by the judge or the jury is how to assign a damage award for the loss of life.

Although there are statutory differences across states, there are some common factors that are looked at to determine the damage award. Two broad categories of factors are damages based on *contributions*, and damages based on *loss to the estate*. The first category primarily deals with the benefits that would have been provided for the decedent's beneficiaries had there been no wrongful death. The second category primarily deals with the probable earnings of the decedent, less probable personal expenses, had there been no wrongful death. Both of these factors focus on the *pecuniary* (or monetary) aspects of the loss, as opposed to the *nonpecuniary* aspects.

From a social perspective, a value of life includes anything that can be considered valuable to the individual. This tends to involve much broader categories than are included in a legal wrongful death damage determination. The goal of estimating of value of life, then, is to try to place a dollar value on both the pecuniary *and* nonpecuniary aspects of that value. How can this be done?

Individuals routinely take actions that suggest they are either willing to pay to *avoid*, or must be paid to *incur*, an increased risk of death. For example, if you buy a smoke detector for your home, you demonstrate that you are willing to pay a certain price to reduce the probability of being harmed or killed in a fire. Conversely, if you decide not to buy a smoke detector, you demonstrate that you are not willing to pay a certain price to be safer. In either case, your action can be used to infer a statistical value of your life.

To provide an example that is illustrative of a common approach economists use to estimate a value of life, let's consider an individual's decision process in choosing a job. Consider the following hypothetical situation. You are trying to choose between two job offers. Both jobs are completely identical to you except in two respects—one job has a slightly higher risk of death than the other job, and the wage rates may differ. Obviously, if you choose the riskier job it must be because you will be paid a wage premium relative to the less risky job. If you choose the less risky job, the wage premium will not be enough to compensate you for the increased risk. In this case, we may be able to identify the exact wage premium that makes you *completely indifferent* between the two jobs. With that amount, and some idea of the difference in the risk factors of the two jobs, we can estimate a value of life.

Let's make up some numbers to demonstrate the technique. Suppose the riskier job has a one in ten thousand (1/10,000) higher death risk than the less risky job. If I were to ask you, what is the minimum annual wage premium you would need to take that risk, how would you answer? If your answer is $500, this information tells me you need to be compensated $500 per 1/10,000 increase in the risk of dying. Now, if we think about 10,000 workers each giving an identical answer to the question, we have a total of ($500)(10,000), or $5 million the workers are willing to pay to face, on average, one death from their group. (We say that there is *on average* one death in the group of 10,000 workers because there is a 1/10,000 chance of dying, but this does not mean there will be exactly one death.) In a statistical sense, then, we can say that one life is valued at $5 million. When I ask my students to perform a similar exercise, I get answers that range from $0 to $100 million. For the students who answer $0 and seemingly place no value on their lives, I try to discourage them from seeking careers as airline pilots.

Asking a hypothetical question about a risk choice that you would never explicitly consider in the real world may not be a very reliable way to determine a value of life estimate. Economists often use a more sophisticated statistical method that involves using labor market data on the determinants of wage rates. A worker's wage depends on many factors such as education, experience, type of industry, union status, fatality and injury risks, and several other things. Fortunately, there is a tremendous amount of data that exists on all of these variables for thousands of workers. A statistical technique allows the researcher, in effect, to compare workers with identical characteristics across every dimension except job fatality risk, and then determine the wage differential for a corresponding risk differential. If it is found, for example, that a $500 annual wage premium is needed to compensate for a 1/10,000 risk premium, the statistical value of life estimate for an average worker is calculated (just as above) to be $5 million.

The main advantage of using labor market data to estimate a statistical value of life is that we are using data based on observable market behavior. We are not asking a hypothetical question. Instead, we are observing wage/risk trade-offs that workers make in determining their optimal employment decisions. We must be careful, however, to take note that it is possible that workers, in general, do not have a good idea about the magnitude of the risks they face. If a worker underestimates the true risk of death, the amount needed to be compensated for accepting that risk *undervalues* the true statistical value of life. Furthermore, workers are not identical. Two workers facing the same risk may require different amounts of compensation. Thus, a statistical value of life found using data from one specific group of workers may not be an accurate value for another group of workers.

There have been numerous empirical studies that have attempted to estimate a statistical value of life. Many of these studies have proceeded along the same lines, but have used numerous different data sets. While it is impossible for all these various studies to reach exactly the same value of life estimate, the range of estimates is generally between $3 million and $7 million. Furthermore, there is a general belief that the typical wrongful death damage estimate usually (grossly) underestimates the statistical value of life estimate found in most empirical studies.

Returning to the Pinto case, the problem with Ford's cost-benefit analysis was not that they were trading lives for dollars. That necessarily must be done in designing products that may be used in ways that create the possibility of injuries or death. From their perspective, Ford correctly determined what they expected their legal liability to be largely based on the $200,000 wrongful death damage estimate that the courts used. However, if the social value of life estimate falls in the lower end of the $3 million to $7 million range, the dollar cost of not adding the safety modification in terms of life lost and injury would be close to $1 billion. This outstrips the $50 million cost estimate used by Ford by a factor of twenty! With the larger value of life estimate, the conclusion of the cost-benefit analysis shows that the additional safety modification would have been cost effective and should have been implemented. Thus, Ford would have had to face a higher amount of liability to provide them with the incentive to add the safety feature. But this was more of an issue for product liability law (see chapter 8) or automobile safety regulation than it was for criminal law. Ford was ultimately acquitted of all criminal charges.

SCARCITY

If you accept the notion that there is a finite value of life for cost-benefit purposes, you necessarily accept the notion of trading lives for dollars. This implies that there are some safety features that simply are not cost effective. But what value of life estimate should you use? If too low a value is placed on the value of life, many safety features would be deemed not cost effective. If too high a value is used, too many safety features would be considered cost effective. But can you ever really have *too many* safety features? If we are not confident in the value of life estimate, shouldn't we at least use a high value so that we bias our results in favor of increased safety? The high end of the labor market estimates is $7 million. Is that the best estimate to use? Why not $10 million, or even $20 million? Let's be extremely safe and go as high as $50 million. In that case, any safety measure that costs less than $50 million per life saved should be implemented. Is this economically sound?

Suppose you are in the position to allocate state health insurance payments and you have to make a choice between spending $5 million to keep a comatose child alive for at most one month, or using the $5 million to give ten sick children life-saving operations. Which would you choose? My mother once gave me a very compassionate answer to this tough question: "I'd keep the comatose child alive *and* give the ten children their operations." That's a very nice answer, but it can lead to a follow up question: What if the $5 million used to keep the child alive for one month can be used to save another ten children? If you answer that you should spend all $15 million, I can ask the same follow-up question again, and again. There will always be trade-offs to consider.

In the very first economics course I took, on the first day of class the professor defined economics to be the study of the allocation of *scarce* resources. If resources were not scarce, we could have practically everything we wanted—there would be few trade-offs to consider. A convenient way to think about resources is to use a monetary equivalent. A value of life estimate is a monetary value, but it corresponds to something concrete—a life. When I talk about spending $5 million to save ten children, the $5 million really refers to the value of the resources used in the life-saving operations. These resources are scarce, and there are only so many resources we as a society can spend on safety, or education, or defense, and so on. Every dollar of resources we spend somewhere is one dollar less we can spend elsewhere. This is why it is important to carefully consider where the dollars are spent, even when considering saving lives.

A value of life estimate is a useful benchmark to use in making safety decisions. For example, a 1985 Federal Aviation Administration (FAA) regulation that implemented an aircraft cabin fire protection standard cost $100,000 per life saved. In this case, pretty much any statistical value of life estimate you use would suggest that the regulation is extremely cost effective. At the other extreme, a 1978 Occupational Safety and Health Administration (OSHA) regulation that implemented an arsenic occupational exposure limit cost $127 million per life saved. Even if you use the very high end of the value of life estimates, the cost of this regulation does not appear to be justified. But what if you simply refuse to accept the concept of a *cost-justified* safety feature? You wouldn't be alone: the U.S. Supreme Court would be standing right behind you!

In a landmark 1981 case involving cotton dust standards, the Supreme Court ruled on the interpretation of the Occupation Safety and Health Act with respect to cost-benefit analysis:

> The Act directs the Secretary to issue the standard that "most adequately assures . . . that no employee will suffer material impairment of health," limited only by the extent to which this is "capable of being done." In effect then . . . Congress itself defined the basic relationship between costs and benefits, by placing the "benefit" of worker health above all other considerations save those making attainment of the "benefit" unachievable. . . . Thus, cost-benefit analysis by OSHA is not required by the statute because feasibility analysis is.

The implication of this ruling is that if a safety feature that reduces the risk of injury to a worker is technically feasible, the cost of that safety feature is not relevant in terms of policy implementation. If you take this ruling literally, why not simply abolish the American cotton industry? This is technically feasible, and it would reduce the risk of cotton dust-related illness to zero. If you believe that abolishing a whole industry for the sake of worker safety is unwarranted, once again you accept the notion that there is a trade-off between lives and dollars. The manner in which you could resolve this trade-off, however, remains the interesting question.

It is unlikely that OSHA completely ignores costs in determining occupational safety standards. The most likely effect of the Supreme Court's ruling is that much more weight will be placed on the benefit of occupational safety features compared to the costs of such features. This may account for why regulations that cost over $100 million per life saved are routinely proposed, and sometimes enacted.

SOME ADDITIONAL THOUGHTS

To end this chapter, I would like to return to the Ford Pinto case to reflect on a few additional points. That case provides an excellent example of the difference between *private* costs and *social* costs. Ford was concerned with the private cost of their decision not to include the additional safety feature, and this cost largely hinged on how the courts assessed the value of life. But if the courts' assessment was well below the true social value of life, Ford's best private decision could diverge from the best social decision. Much of the law is concerned with this problem. If nobody in the world ever bothered anyone else, there would be little need for laws. But individual decisions are often made without explicit acknowledgment, or with poor information, of how one's decision may impact another. One role of social policy, then, is to try to provide incentives for private parties to take into account the social costs they may impose on others. This will be a common theme throughout the book.

The Pinto case also provides an example of how to evaluate a tragedy from a social perspective. The Pinto accident was a horrible tragedy. Three girls were killed and their family and friends were devastated. But a tough question remains: Does the Pinto accident create a motivation for additional social control of automobile safety standards? In this case, the answer may be yes. Ford decided against the additional safety feature because they took into consideration the court-determined liability damages, which may have been a gross underestimate of the true social value of life. In this sense, the accident may have alerted us to reevaluate the social costs and benefits of Ford's decision.

In general, however, many tragic accidents do not rise to the level of a social tragedy. If a train derails and many people are killed, this accident does not necessarily tell us that railway safety standards were inadequate. Regardless of the comprehensiveness of safety standards, there is always a chance that a train may derail. The goal of eliminating all risks of injury or death is a noble one, but simply not realistic. The main reason for this is that the cost of additional risk reductions will, before too long, become prohibitive. But even if you don't consider the costs of additional safety features, in most situations it will be technically infeasible to lower the accident rate to zero short of banning all potentially risky activities.

Trying to determine if a tragic accident rises to the level of a social tragedy demonstrates another aspect of economic reasoning. It is not that economists ignore the substantial costs of a tragedy like the Pinto accident or a train derailment. Quite the contrary. Our goal is to try to measure the costs as accurately as possible, without being biased or overwhelmed by the nature of the tragedy in and of itself. Regardless of the nature of the tragedy, the ultimate question that must be answered in designing social policy for health and safety issues is this: What is the *optimal* accident rate in any given risky situation? The answer to this question must ultimately involve some form of cost-benefit analysis that trades lives for dollars, regardless of how much importance you place on the costs or benefits being considered.

Finally, we have talked about the Pinto case in terms of a technological safety feature. If Ford lacked the proper social incentive to install the feature, we can argue that there is a role for social policy to impose that incentive either through regulation or civil liability through the tort system. But safety is not just a technological problem. Consider more detailed facts of the Pinto case. Before they were hit from behind, the girls were stopped on a highway with no shoulder to retrieve a gas cap they had forgotten to replace after filling up with gas. Are they at least partially to blame for the accident? What about the driver of the van who supposedly was distracted and not watching the road? Was he partially to blame? Technology can only help so much: human behavior is also a big factor in determining the accident rate. Furthermore, improved technological features may adversely affect human behavior, possibly leading to the strange result that additional safety features may actually *increase* the accident rate. I will discuss these issues in later chapters.

NOTES

A leading economic researcher on value of life estimates and the economics of safety is W. Kip Viscusi. There are several excellent sources of his that have contributed to this chapter (and to several other chapters). For an extensive survey, see the article "The Value of Risks to Life and Health," *Journal of Economic Literature* 31 (1993): 1912–46. For a textbook treatment, see W. Kip Viscusi, John M. Vernon, and Joseph E. Harrington, *Economics of Regulation and Antitrust*, 3d ed. (Cambridge, MA: MIT Press, 2000).

Viscusi has also written about the Ford Pinto case in *Reforming Products Liability* (Cambridge, MA: Harvard University Press, 1991). For an interesting general book on the case, see Lee Patrick Strobel, *Reckless Homicide?: Ford's Pinto Trial* (South, Bend, IN: And Books, 1980).

For a legal description of factors considered in calculating wrongful death damages, see Restatement (Second) of Torts § 925: Actions for Causing Death.

The cite for the Supreme Court case on cotton dust standards is *American Textile Manufacturers Institute, Inc. v. Raymond J. Donovan, Secretary of Labor, United States Department of Labor*, 452 U.S. 490 (1981).

3 Do You Want to Trade?

WHILE I was living in College Station, Texas, many years ago, the local newspaper had an interesting article on how smart grade school children can be. A reporter wanted to investigate whether or not young children were eating healthy food. The reporter interviewed children who had in their lunch bags healthy snacks, such as fruit, instead of junk food snacks, and asked, "Do you ever trade your healthy snacks for junk food?" If I remember the story correctly, the children unanimously said, "No." The conclusion was that these children preferred to eat healthy snacks.

I hate to debunk a story about smart children, but there is probably a much simpler explanation for the reason why the children with the healthy snacks were not trading with the children with the junk food snacks. Put yourself in the position of a ten-year-old child with a Snickers bar. Another child approaches you holding a banana and asks you to trade your Snickers bar for the banana. What would you do? My guess is that you would not find it to your advantage to give up your Snickers bar for a banana. It has nothing to do with the other child wanting to eat healthy food. Instead, it has everything to do with you not wanting to trade a candy bar for some fruit.

For trade to occur, both parties must find the transaction to be mutually advantageous. Economists refer to this as *gains from trade*. Let's say I have a used car to sell, and I would sell it as long as I can get at least $3000. If I'm offered anything less than $3000, I would rather keep the car. Assume that there are two potential buyers for my car.

I may have no idea how much each buyer is willing to offer me for my car, but each of them must have some maximum amount that they are willing to pay. Let's say the first buyer is willing to pay at most $2500, and the second buyer is willing to pay at most $3500. With these amounts, the first buyer and I could negotiate for days but we would never come to an agreement. The most buyer 1 is willing to pay falls $500 short of the lowest amount I am willing to accept. Buyer 1 and I have no gains from trade.

With buyer 2 it is a different story. We don't know each other's values, but through negotiation we are very likely to come to an agreement on some price between $3000 and $3500. Gains from trade exist between buyer 2 and me, and the dollar amount of those gains are $3500 − $3000 = $500. This means that at whatever price we agree upon, we will share the $500. The closer the price is to $3500, the greater the share of the gains I receive. The closer the price is to $3000, the greater the share of the gains buyer 2 receives.

One of the key implications of gains from trade is that they allow a resource to be transferred to a *higher-valued use*. If, like many economists, you are concerned with economic efficiency, the objective of moving a resource to a higher-valued use is one that you can embrace. But it must be noted that value is a subjective concept. I value my used car at $3000, buyer 1 values it at $2500, and buyer 2 values it at $3500. There is no right or wrong to these values. They are simply how much each individual, for whatever reasons, subjectively values the car.

The concept of subjective value is central to economic reasoning, yet to the noneconomist it is sometimes poorly appreciated. I believe this is because people often have the tendency to implicitly impose their own subjective values on others. For example, have you ever seen a friend buy something you thought was ridiculously expensive? Did you think to yourself that your friend was being ripped off or maybe just being foolish? But if your friend was willing to pay the price for the product, there necessarily must have been gains from trade from that purchase. Your friend and the seller must have both benefited from the transaction, or else it wouldn't have occurred. You may not have experienced gains from trade from the same transaction, but you weren't the one making the purchase.

I also believe the confusion about the term *value* comes from its common use as a synonym with the word *price*. How many television commercials have you seen that refer to a low price as a great value? But the term *value*, as I'm using it, has very little to do with the price of a product. While the price establishes a minimum value a buyer must have to be willing to purchase the product, the price itself tells us nothing about the maximum amount that buyer would be willing to pay. And it is this maximum amount that establishes a buyer's value for the product.

The concept of mutually advantageous gains from trade provides the main justification for supporting the existence of markets. For example, the used-car market allows me to sell my car to someone who values it more than I do. I don't need to know how much a potential buyer values my car, and the buyer doesn't need to know how much I value my car. The market simply allows us both to take advantage of our gains from trade. This is exactly what the well-known concept of the *invisible hand* refers to. Furthermore, as long as I am free to sell my car to whomever I want to, I will never sell it to someone who values it less than I do. Thus, a market encourages the movement of a resource to a higher-valued use, but prevents the movement of a resource to a lower-valued use.

Unfortunately, the invisible hand is sometimes missing a finger or two. For example, if buyer 2 doesn't know I have a car for sale, we will never get together to exploit the gains from trade. Also, even if buyer 2 knows about my car, it may be too costly for us to physically negotiate a deal. Travel costs, time costs, schedule conflicts, and so on, are all part of a broad category economists refer to as *transactions costs*. If the transactions costs are high, gains from trade may not be exploited. Information costs and transactions costs are often referred to as *market failures,* and are sometimes put forth as justifications for nonmarket alternatives to allocating resources. In some situations, even if no market failure is identified, the concept of a market existing in and of itself is thought of as inappropriate, or even worse.

CELLS FOR SALE

In the 1980s, an important property rights case slowly worked its way through the California court system. *Moore v. The Regents of the Uni-*

versity of California had all the drama of a made-for-television movie. Moore, a patient at the UCLA medical center, had his diseased spleen removed in a life-saving operation. The spleen's cells were then used by his doctors to develop a cell-line that led to the development of several pharmaceutical products. The commercial value of these products was literally in the billions of dollars. Moore was excluded from sharing the revenue and, understandably upset, he sued his doctors. The case was quite intricate, and the court opinions representing the majority and dissenting views in the last two appeals were long and contentious. To make the analysis less complicated, I'm going to tell a simplified (and largely hypothetical) version of the story to illustrate some basic concepts in the economics of property rights.

Let's consider the following facts. A patient is about to have his spleen removed in a life-saving operation. Assume that the doctor informs the patient that it is possible that the spleen may yield some material that can be used to develop pharmaceutical products. If the patient is given the property right over the spleen, the doctor cannot use the material without the consent of the patient. If the doctor is given the property right over the spleen, the patient has no say in how it is used once it is removed. Prior to the operation, a court will determine who is given the property right. You get to be the judge. How do you rule? If you are concerned with the economic concept of getting the spleen to its highest-valued use, the surprising answer is—it doesn't matter. No matter how you rule, you are guaranteed to make the right decision.

What happens if you award the property right to the doctor? The doctor removes the spleen and keeps it. The spleen can be used to develop as many products as possible. The patient gets nothing. End of story. What happens if you decide to award the property right to the patient? The doctor removes the spleen and keeps it. The spleen can be used to develop as many products as possible. The patient becomes filthy rich. End of story.

But haven't we missed something? If the patient is given the property right, how does the doctor end up with the spleen? Ask yourself this simple question: "How long would it take me to sell my already-removed spleen to the doctor, possibly for millions of dollars?" Your answer to that question explains how the doctor ends up with the spleen!

The thought of allowing the patient to *sell* his cells is abhorrent to some. The majority opinion in the first appeal addressed this issue:

> We are told that if plaintiff is permitted to have decision making author-
> ity and a financial interest in the cell-line, he would then have the unlim-
> ited power to inhibit medical research that could potentially benefit
> humanity. He could conceivably go from institution to institution seek-
> ing the highest bid, and if dissatisfied, would claim the right simply to
> prohibit the research entirely. We concede that, if informed, a patient
> might refuse to participate in a research program. We would give the
> patient that right. As to defendants' concern that a patient might seek the
> greatest economic gain for his participation, this argument is unpersua-
> sive because it fails to explain why defendants, who patented plaintiff's
> cell-line and are benefiting financially from it, are any more to be trusted
> with these momentous decisions than the person whose cells are being
> used. . . . If this science has become science for profit, then we fail to see
> any justification for excluding the patient from participation in the
> profits.

There is something about body parts, profits, and medical ethics that does not mix well for some people. The real issue in this case is not where the spleen ends up. The gains from trade are just too enormous for the doctor not to end up with the spleen. The real issue seems to be one of equity. Should the doctor have to pay for the spleen? If, as the judge, your only objective is to move the resource to its highest-valued use, it does-n't matter to you if the doctor has to pay or not. But it may matter to oth-ers, and it will certainly matter to the doctor and the patient.

How was the real case actually decided? In the first appeal, from which the above excerpt is taken, Moore was given the retroactive prop-erty right over his spleen. In the final appeal, however, Moore's prop-erty right was denied. Moore was, for a brief time, a very wealthy man.

In the *Moore* case, the spleen was removed because it was diseased. It's not as if the doctor was trying to cut out a healthy organ for medical and financial gain. It's hard to believe that anyone would argue that, once removed, a diseased spleen should not be used for medical research. But what if the spleen was healthy? As abhorrent as some people find the selling of diseased organs, imagine how some would feel about the selling of healthy organs. What about the selling of organs for transplant from recently deceased individuals? Economists often champion such free-market ideas, despite the moral outrage such market solutions often elicit. To sidestep the usual criticisms of establishing a market for the selling of organs, I'm going to use economic reasoning to take the analysis in a completely different direction.

LEGALIZED ORGAN SNATCHING

There is a severe shortage of organs available for transplant in the United States, and this fact is widely known among health-care officials and many public policy scholars in a number of fields. The current system of supplying organs for transplant by donation only has clearly failed, and there have been numerous suggestions put forth on how to alleviate this shortage. While the various policy options all have a common goal of increasing the supply of organs, the options differ in other goals involving moral, ethical, and legal arguments.

For discussion purposes, I want to examine a policy option that has as its single goal the maximization of the supply of organs available for transplant. I am not claiming that this policy option is in any sense the correct one, or even that I personally endorse it. I just want to present it as a starting point for a discussion of the trade-offs associated with organ transplant policy. So what is this policy option? Nothing less than the forced conscription of all available organs from the recently deceased!

Before you label me a complete nut for suggesting the widespread practice of allowing the medical profession to remove organs from the dead, I'll give you the opportunity to label me a complete nut for believing that theft in almost any context can be economically efficient. Let's return to the used-car example introduced at the start of this chapter. If I value my car at $3000 and a potential buyer values it at $3500, we can exploit gains from trade and negotiate a deal that moves the car from me to the buyer. The gains from trade to both parties involved in a transaction allow a market to transfer a resource to a higher-valued use, and a resource will only be transferred if the buyer's value outweighs the seller's value. A market, however, is still simply a means to an end, with the end being the efficient allocation of resources.

While it can be argued that a market is the best way to allocate resources, the existence of a market is not required to move resources to a higher-valued use. For example, if instead of buying the car, what if the buyer steals the car from me? In terms of the objective of moving the resource to its highest-valued use, stealing the car achieves the same efficient allocation of resources as does selling the car. So, why should we care *how* the resource is allocated to its highest-valued use as long as it *is* allocated to its highest-valued use?

It doesn't take much imagination to quickly point out some of the shortcomings of the efficient-theft theory. First, how can it be guaranteed that theft will always move the resource to a higher-valued use instead of a lower-valued use? What if the person who values my car at $2500 steals it? Second, with legalized theft, individuals are likely to underinvest in property. If I believe my car can legally be stolen at any time, I am not going to be enthusiastic about buying a car in the first place. I'd probably just steal one. Third, individuals are likely to overinvest in resources used to prevent theft, such as locks, alarms, and high-powered rifles. Finally, living in a society where your property can legally be taken from you at any time will undoubtedly upset many people. This is of no small concern. An argument of public outrage against a system of allocating resources may indeed be enough to rule out that system from serious policy consideration.

However, these arguments against stealing may have less impact when considering organ conscription. First, while it is not always the case (such as with religious objections), it is likely that far more often than not organs will be of higher-valued use harvested for potential transplants than they will be if left with the cadaver. This, however, is a sticky point. The great advantage of a market is that the transacting individuals decide for themselves what their values are and whether or not there are gains from trade to be exploited. A strong criticism of nonmarket transactions is that they require a third party to decide where resources are best allocated, and that decision may be incorrect.

A market transaction cannot move a resource to a lower-valued use, but a nonmarket transaction can.

Second, because you are born with your organs, underinvesting in organs is not likely to be a great concern. Of course, to dissuade the system from harvesting your organs upon death, you may decide to abuse them while alive. But choosing to take poor care of yourself *specifically* to depreciate the value of your organs is unlikely to be a serious problem. Third, overinvesting in theft protection is also not likely to be relevant. Granted, you could try to arrange to die in secret so that your organs cannot be harvested, but this behavior would occur far too infrequently to have much of an effect on the supply of organs. Finally, what about the public outrage of organ conscription? When there is a mention of some form of organ conscription in the literature, it is largely ignored due to the belief that there would be a substantial public outcry against organs being harvested without the consent of the deceased or the next of kin. One cannot argue that this outrage would not exist, but one can argue that this outrage could be offset by the benefits of conscription.

The obvious substantial advantage of organ conscription is that it will maximize the pool of available organs for transplant. Although every organ transplantation policy reform has as its goal the elimination of the shortage, no reform other than conscription allows for the possibility of harvesting organs from *every* recently deceased individual. Supporters of a market solution, for example, argue that the shortage will eventually be eliminated through the pricing process. But the downside of a market is that, at times, the movement of a resource to a higher-valued use may *not* occur. Market transactions are not costless, and these costs may prevent the movement of a resource from a lower-valued use to a higher-valued use. If the cost of using a market prevents the exploitation of gains from trade, there is a justification for circumventing the market with some other mechanism, such as conscription.

Thus, if you are interested in allocating resources to their highest-valued use, any mechanism you propose to achieve that goal must confront two potential problems: (1) a resource that has a higher-valued use elsewhere may not be transferred; and (2) a resource may be transferred to a lower-valued use. In both cases, the value of the resource is not maximized. A market for organs, for example, avoids problem 2, but may not avoid problem 1. Conscription, on the other hand, avoids problem 1, but may not avoid problem 2. So, which is the more serious problem—too few efficient transfers, or too many inefficient transfers?

If the ultimate goal is to eliminate the organ shortage, not transferring resources may be the more serious problem. But any policy suggestion that increases the supply of organs may eliminate the shortage. It boils down to an empirical question as to how much the supply of organs will increase under different proposals, and what other policy goals may concern you. Conscription, however, will provide the greatest supply of available organs and is likely to reduce or eliminate the shortage sooner than any other suggestion. Furthermore, conscription is not needed as a long term solution. If the organ shortage can be eliminated, conscription can be replaced with any number of different policies that may provide a better long term solution to prevent future shortages. And as medical technology in the transplant field continues to advance, fewer organs will be needed to maintain an adequate supply. If the current shortage of organs can be thought of as a national emergency, conscription can be thought of as an extreme, but effective, immediate solution, just as military conscription is often thought of as sound social policy in times of war.

But what about the economic downside of organ conscription—the possible transfer of resources to a lower-valued use? Just because you or I believe that far more often than not, organ conscription will transfer resources to a higher-valued use, it is not what we believe that ultimately matters. Value is a subjective concept, and for whatever reason organs may be more highly valued with the deceased than with a potential transplant patient. But there are possible refinements to conscription that may minimize inefficient transfers.

The most common refinement to conscription is *presumed consent,* a policy that assumes that every individual is an organ donor unless explicit action is taken to opt out of the program. Presumed consent is simply the reverse of the system currently in place in which every individual is assumed *not* to be a donor unless otherwise stated. With presumed consent, the potential supply of organs will not be as great as under conscription, but it is likely that individuals with the highest value of maintaining their organs will opt out of donating them.

Similar to presumed consent, another possibility is to allow specifically identified groups (such as religious groups) to be waived from having their organs conscripted, even if individuals do not formally opt out of the program prior to death. Under this system, an individual can opt out of the program only if an acceptable justification is given, unlike under presumed consent where the individual can opt out of the program with no justification.

A third possibility to alleviate the problem of inefficient transfers is to require compensation when organs are harvested. When the state uses its eminent domain power to take property, it must provide *just compensation* to the previous owner. From an economic perspective, just compensation plays no role in moving a resource to a *higher*-valued use. Just as in the car theft example, it is the movement of the resource that is important, not the price paid for it, to maximize the value of the resource. But the simplest economic rationale for just compensation is that it helps discourage the movement of a resource to a *lower*-valued use. Just compensation acts like a budget constraint: to take property, the state must at least pay fair market value, however it is determined. Although fair market value may often underestimate true subjective value, at least just compensation places a minimum value threshold on the taking party. Beyond the economic rationale, just compensation can be thought of as a sensible way to soften the blow of having property taken, possibly reducing public outrage.

Finally, another solution to the problem of inefficient transfers is just to ignore it. No organ transplantation system can be perfect. The current system, and other proposed systems, may encourage too few efficient transfers. Conscription may encourage too many inefficient transfers. It comes back to the question, which problem is of greater concern? Keep in mind, however, that just because there may be a high value on not giving up one's organs for whatever reason, the organs may still be of higher-valued use elsewhere. Organs will not be harvested at the whim of the medical profession—they will be harvested to save lives.

When I teach about the different proposals to alleviate the shortage of organs available for transplant, I always ask my students to vote on which proposal they prefer. Before they vote, I offer a description of each proposal, but I don't present a detailed discussion of their relative costs and benefits. Presumed consent is usually the most-preferred, establishing a market receives moderate support, and forced conscription receives no support at all. This is why I enjoy arguing in favor of conscription, to convince my students that with economic reasoning *any* policy proposal can be shown to have advantages (and disadvantages) relative to other proposals. Forced organ conscription is unlikely ever to be considered sound social policy, and possibly rightly so, but it presents an intriguing example of how an extreme short term solution to an extreme problem need not be considered completely outrageous.

NOTES

The citations for the two appeals for the Moore case are *Moore v. The Regents of the University of California*, 249 Cal. Rptr. 494 (1988), and *Moore v. The Regents of the University of California*, 271 Cal. Rptr. 146 (1990).

The basic idea for the result that a resource will move to its highest-valued use as long as a property right is assigned to either party can be attributed to Ronald Coase. See his article "The Problem of Social Cost" *Journal of Law and Economics* 3 (1960): 1–44. For a more accessible discussion, see any text book in law and economics, such as Richard A. Posner's *Economic Analysis of Law*, 3d ed. (Boston: Little, Brown and Co., 1986).

For an excellent collection of readings that cover virtually every aspect of the debate on organ transplants, see Arthur L. Caplan and Daniel H. Coelho, *The Ethics of Organ Transplants: The Current Debate* (Amherst, NY: Prometheus Books, 1998).

4   *What's Yours Is Mine*

A FEW nights ago, I went to see a movie. When the lights went down, the first image that came up on the screen was that of a man in a baseball cap. He was a movie set painter, and he talked about several of the movies he had worked on. As the short piece progressed, its purpose became clear—it was a heartfelt plea against movie piracy. Unfortunately, seconds after the plea ended, a trailer for *Jeepers Creepers 2* (about a winged man/beast trying to eat a busload of high school students) distracted the audience from breaking up into small discussion groups to further consider the piracy issue. However, I did take note of a web site address that I was able to check out the next day.

Under the heading Why Should I Care? the web site offered four concise reasons as to why I should not pirate movies:

1. *You're cheating yourself.* The more I pirate movies, the more difficult it will be for the movie studios to recoup their investment, and fewer movies will be produced for my future enjoyment.
2. *You're threatening the livelihood of thousands.* The entertainment industry is made up not only of big stars and directors, but also of over 500,000 everyday working people (like the above-mentioned set painter). If fewer movies are produced, many of these people will lose their jobs.
3. *Your computer is vulnerable.* File-sharing computer sites open my computer up to destructive viruses and worms.

4. *You're breaking the law.* Downloading copyrighted movies off the internet is illegal, and it is not difficult for investigators to trace this illegal activity back to my computer. If I am caught, it is possible that I can lose my job, face up to five years in prison, and face up to $250,000 in fines.

It is not difficult to appreciate why movie producers are upset with movie piracy. The more pirated movies that are distributed, the less revenue there will be for movie producers to enjoy. I may be cheating myself if I pirate movies, but I assure you that movie producers are far more concerned with me cheating *them*. What may be more difficult to appreciate, however, is that movie piracy, or copyright infringement in general, may be economically efficient. Then again, it may not be.

A PRIMER ON PRICING

When I taught my health economics course for the first time, because of the interdisciplinary nature of the course I promised my students that I would never draw a supply and demand graph. This was an easy promise to keep until I had to discuss the trade-offs associated with copyright (or patent) law. To properly discuss these trade-offs, I had to explain how, according to economic theory, a firm determines the price of its product. My approach was to explain, in words, the three main factors that *simultaneously* determine a firm's price.

Demand: The Consumer's Willingness to Pay for the Product

As I discussed in the previous chapter, the maximum amount a consumer is willing to pay for a product determines the consumer's *value* for that product. The more a consumer is willing to pay for a unit of the product, the higher the product price may be.

Supply: The Costs of Production

For gains from trade to exist, the maximum amount a consumer is willing to pay for a product must exceed the minimum amount a firm needs to be willing to sell the product. Generally, a firm needs to at least cover its costs of production to reap the gains from trade of a sale. Unfortunately, a comprehensive discussion of the different types of costs of production and how they affect price will have most readers quickly flipping ahead to the next chapter. Instead, I will use a simple hypothetical example and boil things down to just two key concepts—*up-front* costs and *incremental* costs.

Suppose you are a book publisher and you decide to buy a book from an author. If you make a one-time payment to the author for publishing rights, that payment can be considered an up-front cost. In other words, before you even produce one copy of the book, you have already incurred a cost that is now behind you. Ahead of you are the incremental costs of publishing the book, that is, the costs you have to incur to physically produce individual units of the book. These costs will include paper costs, printing costs, possibly marketing and distribution costs, and so forth. For each unit of the book you decide to produce, you must, at a minimum, expect to set a price that covers the incremental cost. The greater you can set your price above the incremental cost, the more gains from trade per unit you can receive. But to decide to purchase the publishing rights in the first place, you must set a price that ultimately will return enough revenue to you to also cover your up-front cost.

Market Structure: The Number of Competing Firms

In general, the more firms there are producing an identical (or very similar) product, the lower the price will be. Firms that don't offer a competitive price can be undercut by their rivals. If there is only one firm producing a product, that firm is referred to as a *monopoly*. Monopoly pricing generally yields the highest price relative to the price from any other market structure.

In a competitive market where there are many firms, price is usually driven down close to the incremental cost of production. For example, assume that as soon as you publish your book and offer it for sale, other firms can use the exact same text and publish their own copies of the book. Because they didn't have to incur the up-front cost that you incurred, the minimum price they can set only has to cover the incremental cost. If, however, you are a monopolist, by definition you face no competitors. Thus, a monopolist can set a price above the incremental cost and earn a per unit profit without fear of a rival undercutting that price.

A monopolist's best price is the one that yields the maximum profit. This implies that a monopolist must be concerned with setting too low a price *or* too high a price. Compared to the profit maximizing price, at a lower price a monopolist sells more units but at a smaller price-cost margin per unit. At a higher price, a monopolist has a higher price-cost margin per unit but sells fewer units. Thus, even a monopolist must be concerned with demand and cost conditions in determining its best price.

COPYRIGHT PROTECTION: A CLASSIC TRADE-OFF

Copyright protection assigns exclusive rights over the sale and distribution of intellectual property to the owner of that property. If you are a book publisher, copyright protection, in effect, gives you monopoly power in the selling of your product. Copyright protection leads to a classic economic trade-off. The benefit of the protection is that it can provide incentives for creators of intellectual property to continue to create. The cost of the protection is that it can lead to monopoly pricing in the selling of the property.

As I discussed above, if you are a book publisher, you ultimately have to earn enough revenue to cover all of your costs. Without copyright protection, it is possible that as soon as you release your book, other firms will immediately copy and sell it. These copying firms are likely to be able to undercut your price because they do not have to be compensated for the same type of up-front costs that you incurred. If you are farsighted, before you ever purchase the publishing rights for the book you will look ahead and anticipate the problem of not being able to ultimately cover your up-front costs. At that early stage, without copyright protection you may decide not to purchase the publishing rights from the author. If this were true for every book publisher, the author would not be compensated and, therefore, may decide not to write the book in the first place. Thus, some argue, copyright protection is necessary to maintain a sufficient level of valuable intellectual property.

The downside of copyright protection is that it creates monopoly power. Assuming that the copyright protection can be enforced, you are now the only one who can legally sell the book (or allow others to sell the book for you). With monopoly power comes monopoly pricing, and that can reduce *social* welfare. But exactly why monopoly pricing reduces social welfare is the important issue.

If I decide to pay $25 for the new Harry Potter book, that implies that I value that book at a minimum of $25. Certainly, I'd like to pay as little as possible for the book. The less I pay the more gains from trade I get. But if I actually purchase the book, I must be getting some gains from trade. On the other hand, if you value the book less than $25, you won't buy it because you wouldn't realize any gains from trade from the transaction. Thus, there are two types of consumers we have to distinguish between: those who purchase the product at the monopoly price, and those who don't.

If I purchase the book at the monopoly price, I am not reducing social welfare. As discussed in the previous chapter, it is the realization of gains from trade that is important for economic efficiency, not how the gains are shared. By raising price above the incremental cost, a firm with monopoly power simply has the ability to reap more gains from trade than does a competitive firm. What is important in maximizing social welfare is that a purchase is made by every consumer who values the book more than the minimum amount at which the firm is willing to sell it. That is, social welfare is maximized when all the potential gains from trade in a market are realized. With monopoly power, this won't occur.

As discussed above, competitive firms generally compete price down close to the incremental cost of producing a unit of the product. If the incremental cost is the minimum amount a firm needs to cover, gains from trade exist for every consumer who values the product more than the incremental cost. Thus, in a competitive market, price competition allows for the realization of all the gains from trade possible in that market, even though the consumers reap all of the gains and the firms reap none. By raising price above the incremental cost, a monopolist creates a gap between the price of the product and the minimum amount needed to produce the product. If a consumer's willingness to pay falls within this gap, there are gains from trade that will not be realized because the price is too high. This loss in gains from trade is the social cost of monopoly power.

DO WE NEED PROTECTION?

The key social argument in favor of copyright protection is that it provides incentives for the creation of intellectual property. But copyright protection is not the only means of providing such incentives. Several factors influence the creation of intellectual property, and if these factors are effective, they can weaken the argument in favor of copyright protection. These other factors include

Poor quality of copies. If poor copying technology leads to copies that are inferior to the original, copying will not be a perfect substitute for the original. Even if the quality of the copies is high, many consumers may still prefer to purchase the original product.

Copying takes time. Because the original producer will be the first to the market, there will be a time lag that can be exploited before copying can take place. This time lag may be enough for the original producer to recoup the up-front cost, and then some.

High production costs of copies. It is possible that the incremental costs of copying exceed the incremental costs of the producing the original. Furthermore, even though it is likely that the copier has fewer up-front costs than the original producer, there may still be up-front costs of copying. These costs make it more difficult to produce copies.

Copying may enhance the value of the original product. It is possible that a consumer's willingness to pay for a product *depends* on the consumer's ability to make copies. For example, libraries subscribe to academic journals and provide photocopy machines for their patrons to use. Without the photocopying technology, patrons may be less interested in the journals and the libraries may be less interested in subscribing to them. If this is the case, the demand for the journal subscription depends on the availability of the copying technology. This enhanced demand can lead to a higher price being set.

Nonfinancial motives for creating intellectual property. Many authors and artists create intellectual property for the joy of being creative. Furthermore, the funding needed to create intellectual property may come from sources other than eventual sales, such as family support, private donations, or public subsidies.

Taken together, these factors can determine whether or not copyright protection is necessary to encourage the creation of intellectual property. The recent legal battle between music companies and Napster over Napster's music file-sharing technology provides an excellent setting in which to illustrate many of these factors.

First, music companies do enjoy some lag time before copying can take place, although that lag time may be very short. In any event, there are still many consumers who prefer the original product. Second, Napster has argued that the file-sharing technology actually enhances the demand for the original product. Potential consumers can sample different songs to determine which compact discs they would like to purchase. Furthermore, even if the original product is not purchased, file-sharing can greatly enhance the demand for live performances and promotional merchandise. Third, it is argued that the vast majority of musicians do not reap much of a financial gain from creating music. For every commercially successful band, there are possibly hundreds of local bands that play music for the love of playing music. There is simply too much music produced for file-sharing to have any significant impact in reducing the quantity or quality of music creation.

Although at this point it sounds like I've been hired by Napster to defend their actions, I will now turn to the (inevitable) other side of the story. The strongest argument in favor of copyright enforcement against file-sharing has to do with the low cost of producing copies.

I remember when the music industry was terrified of the blank audio cassette, just as the film and television industries were terrified of the blank video cassette. Can you imagine how these industries must feel about digital copying technology? Although there is an up-front cost to purchasing the necessary equipment to share digital files, computers have become more commonplace every day. Not only are computers now fairly affordable, they have many uses well beyond music file-sharing. As for the incremental cost of making copies, this is now negligible. It is inexpensive and technically simple for anyone with a computer and access to the internet to participate in music file-sharing. All it takes is one person to make available a file that literally millions of other people can share. Furthermore, while audiophiles may disagree, the average listener tends to find little difference in sound quality between the copy and the original. And as the technology rapidly improves, so will the sound quality of the copy. These arguments suggest that without copyright protection, the music industry may be substantially harmed by file-sharing technology, and this may reduce the quantity and quality of music creation.

The above discussion only deals with the issue of whether or not copyright protection is necessary to encourage the creation of intellectual property. If it isn't necessary, that eliminates the main argument in favor of copyright. But even if it is necessary, that still doesn't deal with the main cost of copyright protection: the creation of monopoly power. The argument for or against copyright, however, does not have to be absolute. There is a legal gray area that allows for copyright protection *and* legalized copying.

IS IT EFFICIENT TO BE FAIR?

Consider the facts of the following hypothetical case, loosely based on a real world case from the early 1970s. A United States government library subscribed to several medical journals and provided free photocopies of articles in these journals to other libraries, government agencies, and commercial organizations. Thousands of photocopies were made and distributed. The publisher of the journals claimed that their copyrights were being infringed, and they filed a lawsuit against the government. The government's defense was that they were not infringing on copyrighted work because the copying was legally protected by a doctrine known as *fair use*.

Fair use allows an individual to legally copy copyrighted work. There are several factors that the courts consider in determining whether or not the copying can be considered fair use:

1. The purpose and character of the use, including whether such use is of a commercial nature or is for nonprofit educational purposes.
2. The nature of the copyrighted work.
3. The amount and substantiality of the portion used in relation to the copyrighted work as a whole.
4. The effect of the use upon the potential market for or value of the copyrighted work.

The economic rationale for fair use is similar to the rationale for organ conscription that I presented in the previous chapter. Fair use can facilitate the movement of a resource, or more accurately a copy of the resource, from one party to another. In the organ transplant example, there exists no current market mechanism for moving a resource from one use to another, and conscription is presented as an *alternative* to a possible market solution. In contrast, the sole purpose of fair use is to allow copiers to *circumvent* an existing market mechanism.

As discussed in the previous chapter, a downside of the market solution is that it may prevent the movement of a resource to a higher-valued use if there is an imperfection in the market mechanism. In the case of copyright, one such mechanism may be the firm's ability to set a monopoly price and exclude certain consumers from the market. This creates a loss in gains from trade. By allowing some consumers to take advantage of the fair use doctrine, the courts, in effect, are undercutting the firm's monopoly power. Consumers who would purchase the good at a competitive price, but not at a monopoly price, can now copy the good without infringing on the firm's copyright. This is a strong economic rationale for fair use.

Another possible market imperfection, also discussed in the previous chapter, is the existence of transactions costs. If it is too costly for some consumers to transact with the firm, gains from trade may not be exploited. Fair use allows these consumers to circumvent the transactions process, thus allowing the resource to move to a higher-valued use. The transactions-cost rationale for fair use is often presented by economists. The question raised is this: If there were a perfectly working market, how would resources be allocated? If this question can be answered, the next step is to impose some alternative to the market solution to try to mimic the outcome of the hypothetical market with no imperfections. Fair use is one such alternative.

In the library case, it may be that the monopoly subscription price for the medical journal was too high for some individuals to subscribe. Alternatively, some individuals may have only valued an article or two, as opposed to a whole subscription. However, transactions costs may have been too high to allow the publisher to transact with individuals for specific articles. The court did consider whether or not some market solution could be set up in which the publisher could sell individual copies, but the majority opinion did not believe such a market could exist. The court reasoned that if certain individuals were excluded from the market, fair use would allow these individuals to get copies of the articles through a nonmarket mechanism. But this raises an interesting question: If fair use only allows *noncustomers* to get copies of the firm's product, why would any firm ever challenge fair use in court? They wouldn't be losing any customers, so why would they care?

In practice, it is very difficult to apply the fair use doctrine to a narrow category of users. A rule that allows only noncustomers fair use, but excludes current customers, would be difficult to enforce. In this case, fair use may allow some current customers to become current copiers instead, and this will negatively impact the firm's revenues. Furthermore, the easier it is to make copies, the easier it is to *sell* the copies, and this can further compete away current customers who may not have access to the copying technology themselves. This is why the factors the courts consider in adopting fair use include whether or not the copying will have a commercial use, and whether or not the firm would be too adversely affected by the copying. But even if the courts explicitly take into account the possible adverse effect of fair use on the firm, the courts and the firm may disagree as to the extent of the adverse effect.

This usually explains why firms challenge the doctrine of fair use even if, in theory, it can be applied in a way that doesn't harm them.

In the real medical journal case, the court allowed the copying to be considered fair use by applying the four factors listed above. Access to medical research through academic journal articles was considered to be extremely valuable not only to the copiers, but ultimately to the public through whatever gains future research would yield. Although many users of the copies would ultimately commercially gain from the research, the copies themselves were not being directly used for commercial gain. Furthermore, although the total amount of copying was immense, the government library did place certain restrictions on individual requests for copies, since it was more difficult to get a copy of a recently published article. Finally, the court did not feel that the publisher was adversely affected by the copying. Because of the self-imposed restrictions the library placed on copy requests, and because many requests were for back issues that were not readily available from the publisher, the court decided that fair use would not greatly reduce the value of the copyright to the publisher.

It should be noted that fair use is not only granted for "educational" uses. When the blank video cassette was introduced, Universal City Studios and Walt Disney Productions sued Sony Corporation, the manufacturer of video cassette recorders. The Supreme Court ruled that home copying of television shows for later viewing (called *time-shifting*) did not substantially harm the studios, and videotaping was considered fair use. Napster, however, did not do as well in arguing that file-sharing constituted fair use. Even if the file-sharing was for personal use, there was a belief that the copies would be substitutes for compact disc purchases, and the music companies would be substantially harmed through lost sales.

DRUGS AND PATENTS

As intense is the debate over copyright protection for books and music, patent protection for (legal) drugs is even more intense. A high price on a book or a compact disc may reduce the gains from trade over entertainment products, but a high price on a life-saving prescription drug may lead to a loss in lives. The trade-offs associated with patent protection mirror the trade-offs associated with copyright protection, so I will only briefly consider patents. But as I discussed in the last chapter, health issues and profit motives don't mix well for many people. Even in the medical journal copyright case, because the copies were used for medical research, the fair use exception to copyright protection was easy for the court to rationalize. Had the library been distributing copies of articles from entertainment magazines, the fair use exception may have been a much tougher sale.

Let's start with the factors that determine a pharmaceutical firm's price for their product. On the demand side, there are several factors that can lead to a high price. First, the decision to purchase a drug may not be made by the consumer of the product, but instead it is often made by a physician. This reduces the importance of price in the consumer's purchase decision. Second, because drugs are used to combat illnesses, the willingness to pay tends to be high. Finally, many consumers have their drug purchases subsidized by insurance plans. To the extent that a consumer doesn't bear the full cost of the drug, the price can be higher.

On the supply side, the cost structure for drug production is similar to what I discussed above: there are up-front costs and incremental costs. In the case of pharmaceuticals, however, the up-front costs can be phenomenal. It is not uncommon for it to cost hundreds of millions of dollars and to take up to twelve years to bring a new drug to the market. The up-front costs include the discovery and development of a new drug. A firm wishing to introduce a new drug in the U.S. market must demonstrate both the safety and efficacy of the drug to the Food and Drug Administration (FDA). The testing procedures are rigorous and make up much of the up-front costs. The incremental costs of drug production, on the other hand, are generally quite modest.

As with artistic intellectual property, ultimately the firm's drug price must be high enough to allow for revenue that will cover all of its costs. If a competitive market structure forces the price close to incremental cost, the firm may not be able to recoup its up-front costs. Patent protection in this case gives the firm some monopoly power and the ability to set a price above incremental cost. But, as I argued with copyright, are there alternatives to patent protection that give a pharmaceutical company the ability to cover all of its costs?

While it may be reasonable to argue that a lot of artistic intellectual property will be created by artists with motives that are not solely financial, you rarely hear that argument applied to pharmaceutical companies. Certainly, there are many medical researchers who sincerely want to improve the quality of life for millions of people, but pharmaceutical companies are primarily profit-motivated businesses. As for copying technology, a drug is a specific chemical entity that can be copied exactly. Once the molecular compound is known, a rival manufacturer can perfectly copy the drug without having to replicate any of the discovery or development procedures. It is true, however, that a new drug can be introduced into the market with a reasonable time lag before it can be copied and marketed, but will the time lag be enough to recoup twelve years of up-front costs?

Another difficulty pharmaceutical companies face is that many of the drugs they discover end up not surviving the development process, or are eventually not approved by the FDA. These drugs may never be marketed, but ultimately *their* up-front costs also need to recouped. In contrast, it may be true that many artistic projects end up not returning a profit, but most projects actually can be marketed to recoup at least part of their up-front costs.

One other problem that pharmaceutical companies must contend with is the difficulty in recouping up-front costs from sales in foreign markets. Probably the most common criticism I see concerning American pharmaceutical companies is that they set higher drug prices at home than they do abroad. This is very easy to explain. Many other countries either offer no patent protection for pharmaceutical companies, or they adopt government price controls for drugs. Generic drug competition forces price down close to incremental costs, and government price controls can do the same. What may be surprising, however, is that higher prices at home may be *beneficial* to Americans.

The key benefit to patent protection is that it can allow a firm to set price above its incremental cost, allowing it to recoup both incremental and up-front costs. If the United States does away with patent protection to match the rest of the world, a pharmaceutical company may have no markets at all in which it can successfully recoup all of its costs. In this case, it may not be profitable to try to discover and develop new drugs. Americans may be unhappy with high drug prices, but those high prices may be the only thing spurring on new drug research. The flip side of the story is that the high prices can lead to the monopoly problem of having some consumers excluded from the market. It comes back to the classic trade-off: the high prices may be necessary to encourage drug production, but the high prices may also create a monopoly social loss.

Patent protection is not absolute. The typical effective life of a patent is twelve to fifteen years. After that, generic competitors can enter the market. Furthermore, current FDA rules make it relatively easy for generic entry to occur almost the same day a patent expires. The question then becomes this: Is twelve to fifteen years too much or too little patent protection? Although this question is very difficult to answer, I will leave you with the thoughts of F. M. Scherer, one of the leading economic scholars on patent protection:

> In the author's considered judgment, a pell-mell march toward regulation of pharmaceutical industry pricing could seriously impair the industry's incentives for investments in new products. Governmental bodies that regulate prices and profits characteristically have a myopic bias. They are inclined toward . . . emphasizing recapture of "excess" profits on the relatively few highly profitable products without taking into account failures or limping successes experienced on the much larger number of other entries. If profits were held to "reasonable" levels on blockbuster drugs, aggregate profits would almost surely be insufficient to sustain a high rate of technological progress. . . . Should a trade-off be required between modestly excessive prices and profits versus retarded technical progress, it would be better to err on the side of excessive profits.

NOTES

The website about copyright infringement with the section titled Why Should I Care? can be found at http://www.respectcopyrights.org.

If you are interested in a more thorough economic discussion of a firm's pricing decision, see any principles of microeconomics textbook, such as the text by William A. McEachern, *Microeconomics: A Contemporary Introduction*, 6 ed. (Cincinnati, OH: South-Western College, 2003).

Alternatives to copyright protection are discussed in William M. Landes and Richard A. Posner, "An Economic Analysis of Copyright Law," *Journal of Legal Studies* 18 (1989): 325–63.

A discussion of the economic issues in the Napster case can be found in a series of papers in the May 2002 issue of the *American Economic Review (Papers and Proceedings)* 92:205–16. The papers are by Benjamin Klein, Andres V. Lerner, and Kevin M. Murphy, "The Economics of Copyright 'Fair Use' in a Networked World"; Michele Boldrin and David Levine, "The Case Against Intellectual Property"; and Paul Romer, "When Should We Use Intellectual Property Rights?" A nice summary of these papers is presented by Douglas Clement, "Creation Myths: Does Innovation Require Intellectual Property Rights?" *Reason Online*, March 2003.

The factors the courts consider in fair use cases can be found at *United States Code Annotated, Title 17, Copyrights, Section 107, Limitations on Exclusive Rights: Fair Use.*

The case cite for the medical journals case is *Williams and Wilkins Company v. The United States*, 487 F. 2d 1345 (1973). The case cite for the blank video cassette case is *Sony Corp. of America v. Universal City Studios, Inc.*, 464 U.S. 417 (1984). The case cite for the Napster case is *A&M Records, Inc. v. Napster, Inc.*, 114 F. Supp. 2d 896 (2000).

Two interesting articles on copyright and fair use are by Wendy J. Gordon, "Fair Use as Market Failure: A Structural and Economic Analysis of the Betamax Case and Its Predecessors," *Columbia Law Review* 82 (1982): 1600–57, and Cynthia M. Cimino, "Fair Use in the Digital Age: Are We Playing Fair?" *Tulane Journal of Technology and Intellectual Property* 4 (2002): 203–21.

For a general discussion of the economics of the pharmaceutical industry, see the text by W. Kip Viscusi, John M. Vernon, and Joseph E. Harrington, *Economics of Regulation and Antitrust*, 3d ed. (Cambridge, MA: MIT Press, 2000), chapter 24. Also see the article by Ernst R. Berndt, "Pharamceuticals in U.S. Health Care: Determinants of Quantity and Price," *Journal of Economic Perspectives* 16 (2002): 45–66.

The quote that ends the chapter is by F. M. Scherer, "Pricing, Profits, and Technological Progress in the Pharmaceutical Industry," *Journal of Economic Perspectives* 7 (1993): 113.

5 *Smoke If You Got 'Em*

To begin this chapter, I am going to ask for your indulgence. Pretend that you don't know that this chapter is about smoking. Instead, let's consider some hypothetical product I'll call X. Product X has been around for a long time. Many people use it. Over the years, a tremendous amount of incontrovertible evidence has been gathered to demonstrate that using X can increase your chance of being harmed or dying. Furthermore, if you use X with your loved ones close by, they too face an increased chance of being harmed or dying. And to make matters even worse, if you use X around complete strangers, you increase their chance of being harmed or dying. Is this enough information to lead you to the conclusion that banning product X may be sound social policy? When I ask my students this question, many of them believe it is enough information. To those students, I then ask them to give me their car keys because product X is not a cigarette, it is an automobile.

Driving is a very dangerous activity. If you take your car out of your garage, you put yourself at risk of harm or death. If you have children and allow them to drive with you, they too are at risk. And let's not forget the dangers you impose on pedestrians, bicyclists, motorcyclists, and other drivers. Driving and smoking have a lot in common. They are both potentially dangerous activities, and they have both attracted the attention of social regulators. If anything, driving is a far more regulated activity than is smoking. So why has smoking been vilified but driving hasn't? You may believe that smoking is far more dangerous than driving, or that smoking has far fewer benefits than driving. As a result, you can legitimately be in favor of banning smoking but not banning driving. But cigarettes have generated a community of hatred against them, unlike any single product legally being sold today.

Smoking is an issue for which I have a difficult time remaining detached. I am not a smoker and, given a choice, I prefer nonsmoking sections in restaurants. From my personal point of view, it wouldn't matter to me at all if smoking were banned from the face of the earth. But professionally speaking, after reading a comment by an antismoking advocate suggesting that there is no role for economic reasoning to play in debating the issue of smoking, I must admit I have come close to adopting an *anti*-antismoking stance.

A few years ago, I was asked by the dean of my college to give a talk at a fund-raising dinner attended by several alumni. Because I am an economist, many of the guests were expecting me to give a talk about the stock market, or the state of the economy. The talk I gave, however, was titled *The Economic Benefits of Smoking*. At first, they thought I was kidding. Every single one of them said they did not smoke, and they couldn't imagine what I could possibly have to say about the benefits of smoking. But after I discussed some of the benefits of smoking, and how some of the costs of smoking may be exaggerated, many of them commented that I had given them something new and challenging to think about. Quite simply, they discovered that economic reasoning *does* have much to add to the debate on smoking.

Actually, it is easy to identify several benefits of smoking, the most important of which is that smokers enjoy doing it. The more daunting task is to argue that there are no benefits to an activity that hundreds of millions of people throughout the world undertake daily. Yet in an exchange of letters published in *Regulation* in 1995, two epidemiologists responded to an economist's article on the benefits of smoking and did just that:

> The disease consequences of tobacco use, ultimately measured in the loss of productive human life, make up the entire risk-benefit picture, unbalanced by concrete benefits.

It is not difficult to use economic reasoning to justify a complete ban on smoking. If you believe that the costs of smoking outweigh the benefits, either due to scientific evidence or just your gut feeling, you may believe that social welfare is maximized by banning smoking. Alternatively, you simply may not care about any benefits that can be attributed to smoking because you do not count those benefits as part of social welfare, even if they outweigh the costs of smoking. But if you argue that there are absolutely no benefits to smoking, you are factually incorrect. This is no longer a debate over the accurate measurement of the costs and benefits, or over the definition of social welfare. You are now, to be polite, unambiguously wrong.

As an economist, the concepts of costs and benefits have been drilled into my head. I can't even think of one term without immediately thinking of the other, even for an activity that is associated with substantial adverse health outcomes, such as smoking. But not all economists approach the issue of smoking in exactly the same way. For example, in a prestigious collection of health economics articles, the authors of a survey on the economics of smoking published in the *Handbook of Health Economics* state the following in their objective:

> The subsequent economic analysis has been motivated by a desire to determine how economic forces influence tobacco consumption, with continued emphasis on refining the scientific rigor of the work: but the objective of much of the research is now to determine how to harness economic forces and logic, how to use economic tools, to decrease smoking, with the ultimate goal being to reduce the toll of tobacco.

And then in a footnote, they add

> Not all of the research is motivated by a desire to decrease smoking. Some authors express the opinion that more respect should be accorded consumer sovereignty, despite the issues of addiction and youthful initiation of smoking that have led many economists to perceive the market for cigarettes as suffering from important market imperfections.

Although the authors do not claim that there are no benefits to smoking, they assume that market imperfections are prevalent enough to allow their analysis to focus on the reduction of smoking as their goal.

Personally, however, I would not relegate the concept of consumer sovereignty to a footnote, and then abruptly dismiss it.

In this chapter, I will work the other way around by initially assuming that smoking is a rational choice for a consumer. *Then,* I will consider the potential market imperfections associated with that choice, such as misinformed consumers, addiction, cigarette advertising, youth smoking, health costs borne by the state, and secondhand smoke. It is likely that most individuals simply would use their common sense to realize that these market imperfections justify a sound role for social policy to control smoking. After all, they all seem so obvious. But I will play devil's advocate throughout this chapter and argue that these so-called market imperfections deserve some serious scrutiny. For now, I will focus on the costs and benefits of an individual's decision to smoke. In the next chapter, I will consider how that decision may be a burden to others.

A MAN ALONE

I want to start off this discussion with an extreme hypothetical example. Let's consider an adult male who enjoys smoking. He is a heavy smoker, and when he smokes he does it completely alone. There isn't even the slightest chance that his smoke will bother anyone else. Also, there isn't a single piece of information about the adverse health effects of smoking that he doesn't fully understand. To put it into economic jargon, he has *perfect information* about the risks of smoking. To complete the picture, he has privately-purchased health insurance to cover any medical expenses he may incur because of his smoking. In the event that he does get ill, he will not be a financial burden to anyone else, including the state. To sum up, he smokes for his own enjoyment, understands the risks of his behavior, and doesn't bother anyone else in any way possible. Do you believe that, for this smoker, there is a justification for the social policy of banning smoking? If you answered yes, I'd like to ask you one more question: Why did you answer yes?

Although I cannot truly explain why you answered yes, I can offer some thoughts on the matter. It is possible for paternalism to justify a social policy against smoking. Even if the smoker has perfect information about the risks of smoking, some believe that it is an acceptable social goal to protect the individual from himself. Putting aside paternalism, another argument can still be offered to justify banning smoking in my hypothetical example. Some people sincerely feel bad when they observe other individuals harming themselves. It's not just that they believe banning smoking will benefit the smoker, they believe that banning smoking will benefit themselves. What role either of these two explanations can play in determining social policy, however, is an open question.

Another possible explanation to why you answered "yes" is because of the extremity of the hypothetical example. It can be difficult to accept an unrealistic hypothetical example, even if it is just used as an intellectual exercise. Smokers don't always isolate themselves from others; smokers are rarely perfectly informed about the risks of smoking; and, smokers who get ill are often a burden to others or the state. So even if somewhere deep down you feel that smoking is an acceptable activity given the boundaries of my example, you don't really accept those boundaries and you implicitly ignore them.

If you believe there is no justification for banning smoking in my hypothetical example, you may still favor social control of smoking when considering more realistic assumptions such as imperfect information, addiction, cigarette advertising, and youth smoking. But how valid are these more realistic assumptions?

WHAT DO YOU KNOW?

My sister used to be a fairly heavy smoker. My father, on the other hand, claims to have never taken a puff of a cigarette in his life. My father was concerned about my sister's smoking habit, and he asked me to talk to her about quitting. I told him he didn't have to worry about my sister's smoking. According to some research on the economics of smoking, if anything she was smoking *too little*.

Before I discuss risk perceptions and smoking, I want to return to the basic concept of gains from trade. If I take out my wallet and pay money for a pack of cigarettes, I absolutely must be benefiting from buying that pack. Any voluntary market transaction necessarily involves gains from trade. Thus, one of the most important benefits of smoking is that of the smoker as a consumer—the benefits as perceived by the smoker must be greater than the price of the pack of cigarettes. When I encounter people who deny the existence of the benefits of smoking, I always immediately ask them to account for why smokers are willing to pay money for something that provides them with no benefits. The usual response I get is that smokers don't understand the risks of what they are doing. Actually, that may be true. There is evidence to suggest that smokers *don't* understand the risks of what they are doing, but it may not be in the way most people think.

The price of a pack of cigarettes is primarily made up of two components—the dollar amount that you have to pay, and a non-monetary amount that reflects the potential adverse health effects of smoking. When you add the two components together, you have what is known as the *full price* of a pack of cigarettes. The concept of a non-monetary price can actually include many other components. If you have to travel to purchase a product, or if you devote time and resources to gathering information about the price or quality of a product, these costs make up part of the full price. Your willingness to pay for the product must outweigh the full price in order for you to realize gains from trade from the purchase of that product. For the sake of simplicity, let's assume that the nonmonetary price of a pack of cigarettes just includes the adverse health risk factor.

To use a simple numerical example, assume that the dollar price of a pack of cigarettes is $3.50 and that each pack imposes a $1.00 risk factor on the smoker. If you are a smoker, and you correctly understand the risk factor, you will only buy the pack if you value it above the full price of $4.50. If you value the pack less than $4.50, you would not get any gains from trade from the purchase. Now let's say you underestimate the risk factor, believing it is only $0.50. If you value the pack above $4.00, but less than true full price of $4.50, you will buy the pack but only because of your misunderstanding of the risk. Had you known the true risk factor, you would not have bought the cigarettes. Thus, underestimating the risk of smoking can lead to too much smoking.

There is also a possibility that you overestimate the risk factor, say at $1.50. In this case, if you value the pack at $4.75, you will not buy it but only because you misunderstand the risk and believe the full price is

$5.00. Had you known the true full price of $4.50, you would have bought the cigarettes. Thus, overestimating the risk of smoking can lead to too little smoking. But what does it mean to smoke too little? It means that if you lived in a world with perfect information, you would not constrain your purchase of cigarettes due to your overestimation of the risk factor.

Individuals may underestimate the risk of smoking, or they may overestimate the risk of smoking. What are the social policy implications of these different types of risk misperceptions? If smokers tend to underestimate the risk of smoking, they are likely to be smoking too much relative to the perfect information world. Underestimation of risk represents a classic setting of market failure, and provides a justification for social policy intervention. What policy is best to reduce the amount of smoking is difficult to determine. Should information be provided that can correct the risk misperception? Or should the activity of smoking be more directly controlled through such policies as cigarette taxation or banning?

If smokers tend to overestimate the risk of smoking, the policy implications can be far more subtle. As an economic purist, I could argue that the role of social policy is to provide the correct information to smokers, suggesting that smokers should be made aware that they are smoking too little. Can you imagine the advertising campaign associated with that idea? The overestimation of the risk of smoking implies that there is already a built-in bias that helps reduce the frequency of smoking. This bias, in some sense, acts in the same manner as a tax on cigarettes. Taxes can be used to reduce the consumption of cigarettes. A possible implication of the overestimation of risk, then, is that the tax rate on cigarettes can be reduced. But for some, anything that increases the rate of smoking, even if the increase is optimal in an economic sense, would be ridiculous. Those in favor of completely banning smoking are unlikely to be swayed by the argument that smokers may not be smoking enough. In practical terms, if smokers overestimate the risk of smoking, maybe the implication for social policy is that we can say there is little role for any *further* policy action.

What evidence is there for the risk perceptions of smokers? It is hard to believe that smokers have no understanding at all of the health risks of smoking. The Surgeon General's warning on cigarette packaging, the antismoking advertisements, and the public condemnation of smoking are all highly visible indicators of the dangers of smoking. Although it is common for nonsmokers to believe that smokers do not understand the risks they are taking, there is some evidence to suggest just the opposite. Some studies show that smokers not only overestimate the risks of smoking, they *grossly* overestimate the risks of smoking.

Contrary to common antismoking messages, smoking doesn't cause bad health outcomes one hundred percent of the time. Smoking may be an unhealthy activity, but it is unhealthy because it increases the probabilities of getting ill or dying. Compared to nonsmokers, smokers have a lower life expectancy, and a higher probability of contracting lung cancer, emphysema, heart disease, and other illnesses. It is these probabilities that appear to be grossly overestimated by smokers, at least according to some research. On the other hand, other studies suggest that while smokers may overestimate the risks of smoking for the general population, they tend to underestimate the risks for themselves. Furthermore, even if many smokers overestimate the risks of smoking, not all smokers do.

Whether or not smokers truly overestimate the risks of smoking remains an open question. The important point is that risk perceptions may play a key role in proposing effective social policy to control smoking. But regardless of the risk perceptions of smokers, antismoking advocates usually point to a much more significant factor associated with the costs of smoking—cigarette addiction.

THE ADDICTIVE CHOICE

Cigarettes appear to be addictive. Perhaps not to every smoker, but definitely to some, and possibly to many. A common view of addiction suggests that it is very shortsighted, nonrational individuals who get hooked on cigarettes. An overly myopic individual will grossly discount the future. In this case, the current decision to start smoking largely ignores any adverse future health effects. This myopic behavior may provide a strong justification for social policy to control an individual's decision to smoke. But what if individuals can make an informed, rational decision to consume a product that may be addictive? Is there such a thing as *rational addiction?*

If you have never heard of the concept of rational addiction, you are probably asking yourself right now, "How can anyone put the words *rational* and *addiction* together?" Then again, after reading about *efficient theft* in chapter 3, you are probably getting used to seeing combinations of words that you rarely see together. Rational addiction sounds pretty abstract, but at its core it is really a very intuitive concept. A rational addict's current consumption depends primarily on two things: past consumption and future consumption. The greater the past consumption of an addictive product, the greater will be the current consumption. The greater the anticipated future consumption of an addictive product, also the greater will be the current consumption. In other words, past consumption and future consumption complement each other—the more of one, the more of the other; the less of one, the less of another.

For example, suppose that the government announces that next year, a significant tax increase will be imposed on cigarettes. If you are a smoker, this will make future smoking more costly for you. If you are a nonrational addict, you may simply ignore the future price increase and maintain your current consumption level. If you are a rational addict, however, you will incorporate the future cost into the current consumption and consume fewer cigarettes *today.* As another example, suppose there is a temporary stressful event in your life that increases your current consumption of cigarettes. As an addict, the more you indulge in smoking today, the more you want to indulge in smoking in the future. This is referred to as the *reinforcement effect.* Thus, as a rational addict, you consider the whole time horizon in your decision to smoke.

The reinforcement effect is at the core of the economic definition of addiction. Often in the literature on addiction, there is a debate about what addiction really means. Is it physical? Is it psychological? Is it a combination of the two? With the reinforcement effect, *any* product can be addictive if an increase in current consumption leads to an increase in future consumption. Cigarettes, alcohol, eating, watching television, shopping on eBay, collecting baseball cards, exercising can all be addictive.

The main implication of rational addiction theory is that addicts are not entirely overwhelmed by their addiction. As with any product, the demand for cigarettes can be influenced by price changes, wealth changes, advertising, new health information, the costs of quitting, and many other things. The thought that an addict must smoke a certain amount of cigarettes every day, without the possibility of adjustment based on the factors just listed, does not stand up well to real world evidence. Every one knows someone who is a *former* smoker. Also, there is ample evidence that smokers respond to price changes, such as those caused by tax increases. Furthermore, rational smokers take into consideration the anticipated future costs of their habit. An often mentioned example of this phenomenon is that when the Surgeon General's report about the adverse health effects of smoking was issued in 1964, over the next decade per capita smoking consumption dropped considerably. Even the smoking rates for young smokers (ages twenty-one to twenty-four) substantially declined, even though they wouldn't be facing the adverse health effects until well into the future.

From a social policy perspective, the justification for controlling smoking behavior is strongest for nonrational addicts. If cigarette addiction leads to serious future health costs, and the smoker irrationally has no concern for incorporating those costs into the current decision to smoke, polices that discourage smoking may ultimately improve the welfare of the smoker. With rational addicts, on the other hand, they optimize over their entire life span. Based on their perceptions of risk, they will consider all the costs and benefits of smoking. In earlier stages of rational addicts' lives, they may find that the benefits of smoking outweigh the costs. As they get older, their cost-benefit calculation may yield the opposite conclusion. Rational addiction boils down to the notion of consumer sovereignty—consumers decide what is in their best interest, even when purchasing products that may be addictive. To the extent that smokers are rational, this presents a weaker case for social policy intervention.

There is one thing that a nonrational smoker and a rational smoker have in common—they both don't appreciate social intervention that curtails their smoking behavior. By definition, a nonrational smoker doesn't consider the future costs of smoking and, as a result, can't appreciate the benefits of policies that may reduce those costs. A rational smoker does appreciate the future costs of smoking and, as a result, doesn't need to be controlled.

Whereas social policy to control smoking is usually thought of as being thrust upon the smoker, new research on rational addiction suggests the possibility that a smoker may *prefer* to be controlled. The intuition of some of this research is that a rational addict may develop a self-control problem. For example, you may decide to start smoking today because of your intention to quit smoking ten years from now. But in ten years, for whatever reasons, you can't bring yourself to quit, and so you regret your original decision to start smoking. If you are aware of this potential future regret, yet still feel that you want to start smoking today, you may welcome social policy that controls your smoking as this will help alleviate your self-control problem.

In all, whatever you believe about the nature and consequences of addiction, it is not likely that any one view of addiction holds true. There are many type of smokers out there. Some are addicts, some are not. Of the addicts, some may be rational, some may not be. Some rational addicts have self-control problems, some do not. Some smokers continually try to quit and often relapse, others never try to quit. The key point is that such tremendous differences in the behavior of smokers make the implications of, and the justifications for, social policy to control smoking much more subtle and complicated.

COMMERCIAL BREAK

When I was a child, there used to be a wonderful television commercial about a cartoon character named Johnny Smoke. Johnny Smoke was a cowboy cigarette who rode into town on his horse. He wore a black cowboy hat and had on a black mask over his eyes. As Johnny Smoke rode by, cowboys with cigarettes in their mouths started dropping like flies. Johnny Smoke was the deadliest killer in the West! It was a dark, eerie commercial, and it made a lasting impression upon me. Possibly because of Johnny Smoke, I have never taken up smoking.

Johnny Smoke was a clever antismoking commercial. Its purpose was to discourage people from smoking. Whether or not it was effective is an empirical question, but its goal was clear. Advertising, in general, is often criticized for doing exactly what it is designed to do—influence behavior. If sound social policy involves curtailing certain types of behavior, it may be sensible to achieve that goal by controlling advertising.

Another common criticism of advertising is that it makes people buy things they don't want or need. This criticism is flawed. Why would anyone buy something they don't want? Unless the advertising is false or misleading, it does not have some magical power to make people spend money on things they don't value more than the price they must pay. What advertising can do, however, is influence someone's value for a product, turning a previous nonpurchaser into a purchaser. In other words, advertising can create gains from trade that did not previously exist. But this brings me back to my earlier point—that is exactly what advertising is designed to do. In short, even if advertising is not villainous, some may think the behavior it promotes needs to be controlled. If you are an antismoking advocate, it is likely that you are against cigarette advertising. But does cigarette advertising really encourage people to either start smoking or smoke more often?

There are numerous empirical studies on the effect of advertising on the demand for cigarettes. Many of the studies find little or no effect of advertising on enhancing the demand for cigarettes, but not all the studies agree. But those who argue that cigarette advertising does *not* affect the demand for cigarettes have the burden of confronting a troubling question: Why do cigarette companies spend hundreds of millions of dollars on advertising?

It may be that the studies that show no effect of advertising on cigarette demand all suffer from some of the difficulties in doing empirical work that I identified in chapter 1. Thus, the results of these studies may be unreliable. It may also be that tobacco companies *believe* cigarette advertising enhances demand, even if it really doesn't. Economists, however, generally don't like to think of people or companies making persistent mistakes, especially expensive mistakes.

Or perhaps cigarette advertising has a different purpose than enhancing the demand for cigarettes. Even if the overall demand for cigarettes is unaffected by advertising, tobacco companies may use advertising as a weapon in brand warfare. In other words, the Marlboro Man isn't interested in potential new smokers, he only wants to shoot it out with Joe Camel. Advertising may be used to fight for market share, even if the size of the overall market is stable or declining over time.

Ironically, if it is the case that all cigarette advertising is for brand warfare, a total ban on cigarette advertising may be *beneficial* to the tobacco industry. If advertising simply maintains the status quo in market shares, it is ultimately ineffective and the tobacco companies would save a lot of money by not advertising. But this wouldn't last for long because each brand would have an incentive to start a big advertising campaign against its rivals. If advertising is banned, however, the government in effect allows the tobacco industry to eliminate wasteful advertising without worrying about individual brands unilaterally increasing their advertising expenditure.

In an environment of substantial antismoking messages, cigarette advertising may be nothing more than an attempt to keep the cigarette market from collapsing too quickly. If this is true, cigarette advertising bans may reduce cigarette consumption, but the precise types of social controls used will determine the effectiveness of the bans. For example, some antismoking advocates have been calling for Hollywood to ban smoking by actors in movies and on television. Although I have seen no evidence of how effective this policy would be in reducing cigarette consumption, I doubt it would have much of an effect.

Some recent studies have argued that partial bans, like the banning of cigarette advertisements on television and radio, are ineffective. Tobacco companies still have plenty of print media outlets to use, and there are several other forms of promotional avenues such as retail display cases, coupons, sporting or entertainment endorsements, and so on. There is some evidence to suggest that a *comprehensive* ban on cigarette advertising may have a substantial effect on reducing cigarette consumption. But even if this was true, there still is the issue of whether or not further controls to reduce smoking is sound social policy.

YOUTHFUL SMOKING

Teenagers have it rough. So many activities that adults take for granted are strictly controlled for teenagers. While the debate over controlling adult smoking is often heated, there tends to be much more agreement (at least among adults) when it comes to controlling teenage smoking. Yet all of the arguments introduced above for adult smokers can also be applied to teenage smokers.

There is some evidence that teenagers also overestimate the risk of smoking, believing that smoking is more risky than it really is. It is also likely that at least some teenagers are rational in the sense that they take into account the future costs of smoking, although teenagers tend to be more myopic than adults. Furthermore, cigarette advertising may have a slightly greater effect on teenagers, but there is still evidence to suggest that their cigarette consumption may not be significantly influenced by advertising expenditure.

There is one more important similarity between teenagers and adults—they both receive gains from trade from purchasing cigarettes. Teenagers are consumers in exactly the same way adults are consumers. A teenager must value a product more than its price to be willing to buy it. Again, we've returned to a consumer sovereignty argument. But this argument has its shortcomings with teenagers. At what age do we believe teenagers can make informed decisions about the products they value, especially potentially harmful products? Many may agree that a seventeen- or eighteen-year-old may be old enough to decide what's best to purchase, but hardly anyone would think the same way for a thirteen- or fourteen-year-old.

If you are in favor of banning smoking for everyone, the best way to control teenage smoking is not much of an issue for you. If you believe adults should be allowed to smoke, but not teenagers, you are likely to favor a social control policy specifically directed at teenagers. One of the most common of such policies has been to set a minimum age limit for the purchase of tobacco. Although this policy has a common sense appeal, evidence suggests that the lax enforcement of the standard at the retail level has greatly undermined its effectiveness in reducing teenage smoking. And while it has been suggested that the policy can be effective if it is rigorously enforced, one must keep in mind that the administration costs of effective enforcement may be huge: there are a lot of cigarette retailers out there. Furthermore, it should also be taken into account that rigorous enforcement of the age standard may just encourage teenagers to become more clever in finding alternative ways of acquiring cigarettes.

Another policy to deter teenage smoking has to do with restricting the promotional activities of tobacco companies, especially with promotions aimed at the youth market. But if it is the case that a teenager's decision to smoke is not significantly influenced by cigarette advertising or other marketing strategies, promotional restrictions may have only a marginal effect on controlling teenage smoking.

The most common social control policy to deter smoking is taxation, but an increased tax rate affects all smokers, not just teenagers. Still, there is evidence to suggest that increased taxation reduces cigarette consumption by at least some amount, and this effect may be larger for teenagers than for adults. But some recent research has taken a closer look at the differential effects of cigarette taxation on teenagers and adults.

Adults and teenagers who are *current* smokers appear to respond in an identical manner to increased taxation: they consume fewer cigarettes. The key distinction to make is between current smokers (at any age) and those who have *not yet* started to smoke. Once an individual is a smoker, taxation can reduce cigarette consumption. What one recent empirical study finds, however, is that cigarette taxation has virtually no effect on reducing the *onset* of smoking for teenagers. While this is only a single study, as more empirical studies of this sort are undertaken we may develop a better understanding of the effectiveness of taxation in controlling smoking.

If marketing restrictions, age limits, and taxation all have limitations in how effective they can be in controlling teenage smoking, is there a more effective control that can be identified? Some argue that there is already a perfect control mechanism in place for teenage smoking that does not involve any social policy intervention—parental control. There is some evidence to suggest that a strong influence on teenage smoking is whether or not parents allow smoking in the home. If parental control is effective, there may be little role for social intervention. But others argue that some parents lack that ability to control their children, especially outside of the home. There is also evidence to suggest that parents are not well-informed about the smoking behavior of their children. Thus, an argument in favor of social intervention is that it makes up for a lack of effective parental control. But then we end up where we started: Exactly what is the best way to control teenage smoking?

If social policy to control teenage smoking is directed specifically at teenagers, the fact that smoking will remain legal for adults will make it that much more difficult for the policy to be effective. Perhaps in the end, maybe the best argument in favor of a comprehensive antismoking policy is that it may be the most effective way to control teenage smoking, and this is a policy objective that many people share. But such a comprehensive policy will have a downside in that it will infringe on consumer sovereignty, which is a concern of at least some people, even if they are mostly smokers and economists.

The prevention of teenage smoking may present the strongest justification to control an individual's decision to smoke. But there are many who believe that the absolute strongest (and possibly irrefutable) argument in favor of a social policy to control smoking is to protect others from being harmed by smokers. It is one thing to bear your own risk, but an entirely different thing to impose a risk on others. In the next chapter, I will examine this argument.

NOTES

The quotation about the lack of concrete benefits of smoking can be found in an exchange of three letters to the editor in *Regulation* 18, no. 4 (1995): 5–7.

The survey article "The Economics of Smoking," is written by Frank J. Chaloupka and Kenneth E. Warner, and can be found in *Handbook of Health Economics*, ed. Anthony J. Culyer and Joseph P. Newhouse (Amsterdam: Elsevier, 2000), 1541–1627. This survey provides a thorough introduction to many of the topics discussed in this chapter, such as rational addiction, cigarette advertising, and teenage smoking. The survey also provides an extensive list of references.

Evidence on smokers' risk perceptions is presented in W. Kip Viscusi, *Smoke-Filled Rooms* (Chicago: University of Chicago Press, 2002), chapter 7.

The seminal article on rational addiction is by Gary S. Becker and Kevin M. Murphy, "A Theory of Rational Addiction," *Journal of Political Economy* 96 (1988): 675–700. For an updated discussion, see Jonathan Gruber and Botond Koszegi, "Is Addiction Rational?: Theory and Evidence," *Quarterly Journal of Economics* 116 (2001): 1261–1303.

The study of cigarette taxes and the onset of teenage smoking is by Philip DeCicca, Donald Kenkel, and Alan Mathios, "Putting Out the Fires: Will Higher Taxes Reduce the Onset of Youth Smoking?" *Journal of Political Economy* 110 (2002): 144–69.

For an overview of the issues in dealing with youth smoking, see Joni Hersch, "Teen Smoking Behavior and the Regulatory Environment," *Duke Law Journal* 47 (1998): 1143–70.

For an interesting and accessible debate on some of the main smoking issues, see the series of articles in *Regulation* 25, no. 4 (2003): 52–72. The articles are by Jonathan Gruber, "Smoking's Internalities"; W. Kip Viscusi, "The New Cigarette Paternalism"; Thomas A. Firey, "My Future Self and I"; and Gio Batta Gori, "Less Hazardous Smokes?"

6 *Stop Bothering Me*

A factory's production process emits smoke pollution into the air. An oil tanker transports oil and, due to an accident, spills oil into the ocean and along the coast. Airports have takeoff and landing patterns that disturb neighboring residents. Secondhand smoke causes cancer in nonsmokers. People talk in movie theaters. Your roommate's television is too loud. This opening paragraph is starting to annoy you. Each of these situations provides an example of what economists refer to as a *negative externality*. Or more simply put: people hate to be bothered.

A negative externality is when an individual's private action imposes a cost on another individual. For example, the owner of a factory may only be concerned with selfishly maximizing profit and not with the consequences of the pollution emitted into the air. Thus, private actions may impose *social* costs, and laws and regulations are often designed to control these costs. But the concept of a negative externality can be extremely broad, and what type of externalities deserve the attention of social regulators can be an intriguing question.

I often present my students with the following two scenarios and ask them if, from a social policy perspective, the two differ. In the first scenario, it is two in the morning and your neighbors are having a loud party and the noise is keeping you from getting any sleep. In the second scenario, it is two in the morning and your neighbors are having a quiet party that is keeping you from getting any sleep because you are upset that you weren't invited. In both scenarios, your neighbors are imposing a negative externality upon you by keeping you from sleeping. Do you believe there is a difference between the two settings?

When I pose that question to my students, they usually claim that there is a difference. In the first case, you are being physically bothered by an identifiable noise. If the party is loud, anyone can observe there is a possibility of an externality. It may be extremely difficult to determine the extent of the externality (in terms of a dollar equivalent), but designing a social policy to stop loud parties is certainly feasible. In the second case, the externality is not easily observed by others. Your hurt feelings can only be verified by you, and this provides a very difficult justification for social intervention. But from a theoretical perspective, I contend that there is little difference between the two settings. The externality of the ongoing party is that you can't sleep. One is a *physical* externality, that is, the loud noise keeps you awake. The other is a *psychic* externality, that is, your feelings are being hurt. The key point, however, is that in both cases you are being hurt.

For the most part, legal cases in which damages may be assessed deal with physical externalities. This makes good sense because physical damages are more likely to be measurable than are psychic damages. But psychic externalities motivate a lot of social policy. In chapter 3, I discussed organ conscription for transplant purposes. When this policy option has been raised, it is usually quickly dismissed by most commentators as being immoral. Developing a market for the selling of organs also is often dismissed for the same reason. Many people against these policies would not be physically harmed by their adoption, yet they are still deemed offensive. Other examples include so-called victimless crimes such as drug use, gambling, and prostitution that are often praised for being illegal by individuals who are never physically affected by any of these activities. This chapter will be devoted to physical externalities, and will eventually focus on the issue of secondhand smoke. But I think it is worth keeping in mind that social policy can be motivated by many factors.

THERE GOES THE SUN

Can anyone own the sun? This seemingly ridiculous question has, in some sense, been at the heart of several lawsuits, including the following two. In a 1959 case, two neighboring luxury hotels in Florida went to court to settle a property dispute. The Fontainebleau Hotel began constructing a fourteen-story addition that, when completed, would cast a shadow in the afternoon over the swimming pool and sunbathing area of the Eden Roc Hotel. The Eden Roc Hotel wanted the right to prevent the additional construction, claiming that the blocking of the sunlight would adversely affect their business by reducing their guests' enjoyment. In a 1982 case, the owner of a solar heated house, Prah, sued the owner of a neighboring property, Maretti, who was building a house. Maretti's house, when completed, would block the sunlight from reaching Prah's solar panels and prevent the solar heating system from being effective. In both cases, the ultimate question to be addressed is this: Does one party have the right to block sunlight from reaching the other party?

When I ask my students to resolve these cases, the general feeling they convey is that the Fontainebleau Hotel should have the right to build the addition, but Maretti should not have the right to build his house. The reasoning offered is that blocking sunlight from reaching a swimming pool and sunbathing area is not that important, but blocking sunlight from reaching a solar heated house is important. At this point in the lecture, I have to congratulate my students. With no knowledge of how the real world cases were decided, my students exactly matched the reasoning used by the courts in settling the real disputes.

In the Prah case, the court argued that

> access to sunlight has taken on a new significance in recent years. In this case the plaintiff seeks to protect access to sunlight, not for aesthetic reasons or as a source of illumination but as a source of energy. Access to sunlight as an energy source is of significance both to the landowner who invests in solar collectors and to a society which has an interest in developing alternative sources of energy.

This reasoning, in part, led to Prah winning his case. The earlier case, however, was lost by the Eden Roc Hotel. Do you agree with my students and believe these were the right decisions? I do, but only because

I don't think it mattered at all how the courts decided either of these cases. But before I explain that, I'd like to examine the court's reasoning behind the Prah decision.

At first blush, it sounds correct that sunlight is more important for energy purposes than it is for aesthetic purposes. Does it really matter that the Eden Roc's guests will have less sunlight for swimming and tanning purposes? The answer is yes, it does matter. If part of the attraction of staying at the Eden Roc is the location of the pool and sunbathing area, lack of sunlight will diminish the Eden Roc's value to its guests. This loss in value could translate into substantial lost profit to the Eden Roc. In other words, the Eden Roc values the sunlight hitting the pool area, and if the sunlight is blocked, the Fontainebleau is imposing a negative externality on the Eden Roc. The court in the Prah case may not value sunlight for aesthetic purposes, but it is not the court that is incurring that externality. One can just as easily argue that there is little value to solar energy given that there are alternative heat sources that Prah can use.

More substantially, the court in the Prah case is making the wrong comparison. It doesn't matter at all how the value of the sunlight to a homeowner compares to the value of the sunlight for a hotel. The homeowner and the hotel do not have conflicting interests. The key comparison in each case is the value of the sunlight to one party versus the value of blocking the sunlight to the other party. If we consider the goal of allocating resources to their highest-valued use, determining the highest-valued use is at issue in each case. Fortunately, that determination may never have to be explicitly made.

Let's make up some hypothetical numbers for ease of explanation. Assume that the Eden Roc values the sunlight at $1 million, and the Fontainebleau values the extension that blocks the sunlight at $2 million. Furthermore, assume that the court has no idea of what either of these values are. How should the court decide? It doesn't matter. Regardless of their decision, the extension will be built. If the court rules in favor of the Eden Roc, the Fontainebleau will be willing to pay up to $2 million to build the extension. Because the Eden Roc only needs at a minimum $1 million, there are *gains from trade* that can make both hotels better off if the extension is built. Exactly how the gains from trade are shared depends upon the relative bargaining strengths of the two hotels. But it is in both of their best interests to have the extension built. What if the court rules against the Eden Roc? The exact same result will occur. The Fontainebleau Hotel will build its extension unless the Eden Roc can pay them at least $2 million not to build. But with the Eden Roc's value at only $1 million, there are no gains from trade to prevent the extension from being built. In either case, the highest-valued use ends up being realized.

If we were to switch the numbers around, giving the Eden Roc the higher-valued use of $2 million and the Fontainebleau the lower-valued use of $1 million, it still wouldn't matter what the court decides. The gains from trade would lead to the extension not being built, which is now the higher-valued use. If the court rules in favor of the Eden Roc, the Fontainebleau would not be willing to pay $2 million to build its extension. If the courts ruled in favor of the Fontainebleau, the Eden Roc would be willing to pay at least $1 million (and at most $2 million) to keep the extension from being built. All the court has to do is give one of the two parties the property right over the sunlight. After that, the parties can negotiate their way to the efficient outcome.

An identical analysis can be used for the Prah case. Whoever has the highest-valued use will end up having their way, whether or not they are awarded the property right or if they have to pay the other party. Both of these cases are also similar to the Moore case (from chapter 3) involving the doctors profiting from taking their patient's cells. In that case, I argued that the gains from trade were so phenomenal that it wouldn't matter what the court did—the cells would eventually end up in the hands of the doctors. The doctors would either have the right to take the cells without paying compensation, or the patient would have the right to sell his cells.

Throughout all of these analyses, though, I am assuming that the parties will actually negotiate to resolve their dispute once the property right is set. In the Moore case, this is almost guaranteed given that there were hundreds of millions of dollars to be shared. But what about more modest cases, like Fontainebleau or Prah, where the gains from trade may be anywhere from hundreds of thousands of dollars to just thousands of dollars? If, for whatever reasons, the negotiation costs are high, the parties may not be able to exploit the gains from trade. What can the courts do in these cases?

THERE'S NO TALKING TO SOME PEOPLE

When two parties refuse to negotiate with each other, the highest-valued use of a resource may not be achieved. The fact that the two parties are in court seems to suggest that they are not working out their problems in the first place. But there are two separate issues here. In the hotel case, the two hotels were not working out their problem because there was a lack of a *well-defined property right.* The Eden Roc didn't actually have the right to unrestricted sunlight, just as the Fontainebleau didn't actually have the right to block the sunlight. If neither party can recognize that one of them does have the well-defined right to some action, how can negotiation take place? So, the first issue is to establish a well-defined property right, which means that the court can make it clear which party has the right over the sunlight. In the hotel case, the Fontainebleau was given the right to build the extension. In the solar energy case, Prah was given the right to stop Maretti from blocking the sunlight.

Once a property right is established, the second issue the court must deal with is how that right should be protected. One simple way to protect a property right is to use a *property rule.* What this entails is, in effect, absolutely nothing. A property rule indicates that the court will not offer any further intervention after the property right is assigned. With a well-defined right, the parties are left to their own devices to work out whatever problems they may have. Once the Fontainebleau is given the right to build the extension, the only way to prevent them is for the Eden Roc to negotiate an agreement not to have the extension built. This will only occur if the Eden Roc values the sunlight more than the Fontainebleau values the extension, *and* if the two parties are willing to negotiate.

When negotiation costs are high, and parties are unlikely to negotiate, a property rule may not achieve the efficient outcome. Unless the court knows the highest-valued use and assigns the property right to that party, there is no guarantee that the highest-valued use will be achieved.

If the court assigns the right to the lower-valued use, and no further negotiation will take place, an inefficient outcome will result. Thus, a property rule coupled with high negotiation costs may not be efficient.

Another way to protect a property right is to use a *liability rule.* After assigning a property right, the court can set a damage payment schedule that can allow one party to affect the actions of another party. For example, assume in the hotel case that the court knows the Fontainebleau values the extension at $2 million, but does not know what the value of the sunlight is to the Eden Roc. Thus, the court does not know what the highest-valued use is. Unless the court luckily assigns the property right to the highest-valued use, using a property rule in this case may not lead to the efficient outcome if the parties won't negotiate. Instead, the court can use the limited information it has to achieve the efficient outcome. The court knows what the Fontainebleau's value is, so it should assign the property right to them. But now, it can allow the Eden Roc to prevent the building of the extension only if they pay the Fontainebleau $2 million. A liability rule that dictates the payment schedule allows for one party to influence the behavior of another party without any negotiation. If the Eden Roc values the sunlight at more than $2 million, it will be worth paying the $2 million to keep the extension from being built and that would be the highest-valued use. If the Eden Roc values the sunlight at less than $2 million, it will not pay and the extension will be built, and now that would be the highest-valued use.

Although the sunlight examples are fairly simplistic, you can apply the above economic reasoning to any negative externality setting, such as those presented in the opening paragraph of this chapter. To the extent that individuals can negotiate, the assignment of the property right is the key aspect of resolving a negative externality. If the parties can't (or won't) negotiate, a property rule can only work if the efficient outcome is known. If the efficient outcome is not known but some information is available, a liability rule may allow for the efficient outcome to be achieved. If no information at all is available, it is very difficult to efficiently resolve a negative externality.

Of course, what is meant by the efficient outcome will depend on the definition of social welfare. For example, in the case of secondhand smoke, the efficient outcome may involve some trade-off between the benefits smokers receive and the costs they impose on nonsmokers. Or, if you are an antismoking advocate, you may support a complete ban on smoking in public places because you don't count the benefits smokers receive as part of social welfare. The issue of secondhand smoke provides more than just an abstract example, however, as it is one of the most contentious negative externality issues currently facing society.

SMOKE GETS IN YOUR EYES AND NOSE AND THROAT

One day, I was sitting in a restaurant with my father and for some reason we started talking about smoking in public places. My father is a rabid antismoker, and he believes there are absolutely no benefits to smoking. This is understandable as he has seen several of his friends who were lifelong smokers become ill or die. Needless to say, he was arguing strongly in favor of banning smoking in public places. Just for fun, I decided to take the opposite position. When I returned home after the meal, I told my mother about the conversation I had with my father, expecting her to side with me. To my great surprise, my mother agreed with my father. After over fifty-five years of marriage, I guess it was bound to happen at least once. Although my father was unyielding to my arguments, I decided to use one of my favorite arguing techniques with my mother—the hypothetical situation.

Let's say my mother is hosting a bridge party at her home, and she invites several friends to attend. Some of her friends happen to be smokers, and others are nonsmokers. What are the possible scenarios? My mother can decide that no smoking is allowed in her home. Her smoking friends can either not smoke or go outside to smoke. Alternatively, they can simply not play bridge. Now let's say my mother decides that it is okay for anyone to smoke in her home. Her nonsmoking friends can put up with the smoke, not play bridge, or ask the smokers to refrain from smoking. Either everyone will come to some mutually agreeable solution, or there will be no bridge game. I asked my mother the following question: "Would you want the government to tell you that if you are going to invite people into your home, you must have a nonsmoking home?" She immediately replied, "Of course not!" *Then* I asked her how she would feel if she owned a restaurant and the government told her she couldn't allow her customers to smoke? I think she appreciated the point I was making. Actually, I think she just needed any excuse to once again disagree with my father.

In the smoking/antismoking war, there may be no greater battleground than the issue of banning smoking in public places. Many nonsmokers may not care if smokers want to make the private decision to smoke, but when it comes to secondhand smoke (also called environmental tobacco smoke, or ETS) there is no such acceptance. Although there is a substantial scientific debate about the health effects of ETS, for now I'm going to assume that secondhand smoke does create adverse health effects in nonsmokers. But just as with most pollution examples, it is not difficult to accept that one person's actions can impose costs on another person. The difficult question involves the appropriate trade-off between the polluter and the victim.

Unlike the examples involving the two hotels or the two neighbors, it is extremely unlikely that smokers and nonsmokers will generally be able to negotiate a solution, even if the property right is well defined. Negotiations may be possible in situations like the bridge party example, or with roommates, but in settings involving strangers there appears to be little room for market solutions to be effective. This may help explain why there is a loud outcry against smoking in public places, and why many localities are banning smoking in bars and restaurants. But despite the fact that patrons of these establishments may not be able to negotiate mutually agreeable outcomes, it does not mean that a market mechanism does not exist.

Exactly what is *public* about a restaurant or bar? If a restaurant is privately owned, there may be nothing at all about it that is public. Granted, restaurants allow complete strangers to come in off the street and be customers, but the decisions made by the restaurant with respect to menu, atmosphere, opening and closing times, and so on, are strictly privately determined. Of course, restaurants are subject to all sorts of social controls involving health and safety issues, and the state can impose smoking bans, but the point I want to make is that a market mechanism does exist to deal with smoking. The mechanism may not be perfect, and ultimately social control may be warranted, but I believe the market mechanism is worth considering.

A private restaurant relies on its customers to stay in business and make profit. Probably the most important decision a restaurant makes involves the menu and the prices, but location, parking, atmosphere, and other factors also affect patronage. A restaurant that does not allow smoking may be unattractive to smokers. A restaurant that allows smoking anywhere may be unattractive to nonsmokers. A restaurant that has a separate smoking section may be able to strike a balance between smokers and nonsmokers.

The restaurant business is generally highly competitive. Restaurant owners can compete for customers across many dimensions. If the smoking policy is a key competitive weapon, the market may easily sort itself out by naturally allowing for restaurants to simultaneously exist with different smoking policies in place. Smokers and nonsmokers can decide which restaurants to choose based on whatever criteria they deem important. Is this any different than a restaurant that is deciding to serve only meat dishes, only vegetarian dishes, or a mixture of the two? Most people would say of course it is: menu items can't kill you!

Is it all, then, a matter of the *degree* of the externality? Is banning smoking in restaurants warranted because smoking is dangerous to nonsmokers? Let's say secondhand smoke instantly kills nonsmokers. Even in this extreme case, social intervention may not be necessary because market forces would likely give restaurant owners strong incentives to ban smoking. But if restaurant owners still refused to ban smoking, would social intervention be warranted? Maybe not.

I have a friend who is a serious antismoking advocate. My friend loves music, especially live music in small venues like bars. Unfortunately, he is extremely asthmatic and can't survive in a smoky bar for more than a few minutes. He once offered me a very compelling argument as to why smoking in bars should be banned. If the main attractions of going to a bar are drinking, listening to music, and socializing with other patrons, a nonsmoker who is severely bothered by smoke cannot enjoy all these activities. However, a smoker still can enjoy these activities, but cannot smoke while enjoying them. Smoking will have to be done outside or not at all. Thus, allowing smoking excludes some patrons from all of the main activities a bar has to offer, but banning smoking only prevents customers from smoking while in the bar. This argument not only appears to justify banning smoking in bars, it elegantly appeals to common sense. But it still does not definitively resolve the debate.

Any externality requires the participation of at least two parties—the polluter and the victim. Although the polluter bears the burden of being the one who actively creates the pollution, the victim must actually be affected for an externality to exist. This suggests that there can be at least two crude ways of preventing an externality: one way is to prevent the polluter from polluting; the other way is to relocate the victim. If all the people who are bothered by secondhand smoke don't go to restaurants or bars that allow smoking, there will be no negative externalities in those restaurants. The cost of that behavior is the lost value from not being able to patronize certain restaurants and bars. Banning smoking, on the other hand, also eliminates the negative externality, but at the cost of the lost value to smokers who will not be able to smoke at will. Determining which lost value is greater can be an extremely difficult thing to do.

Another interesting argument in support of smoking bans in restaurants and bars is the belief that such a ban would be financially beneficial to those establishments. A British newspaper recently reported that

> smoking bans in British pubs and restaurants could drive up profits by encouraging more people to eat out, says the TUC (Trades Union Congress) in a new report that will fuel pressure for greater curbs on cigarettes (*Observer*, May 4, 2003).

This type of thinking can be very annoying to an economist. When I discuss this argument with my students, it usually takes no more than a few seconds for some student to ask, "If restaurants and bars can make more profits by banning smoking, why haven't they done so already?" Exactly! I guess one could argue that the countless number of restaurants out there that permit smoking have just never figured out how unprofitable that can be. If that is the case, the "studies" that show how profitable smoking bans can be should perhaps be persuasive enough to eliminate the need for any form of social control.

Yet another argument for banning smoking, especially in bars, is to protect the *employees* of these establishments, as opposed to protecting the nonsmoking patrons. This is a clever argument, and it has been the driving force behind several antismoking initiatives. One may accept the argument that nonsmoking customers can refuse to patronize establishments that allow smoking, but when it comes to employees there often is a sense that these workers are somehow trapped in their jobs. If workers are forced to inhale secondhand smoke, they are adversely affected at no fault of their own. The problem with this reasoning is that there is no compelling evidence that workers who are unsatisfied with certain job conditions can't find other jobs. Secondhand smoke is only one aspect of working conditions. Employees must consider salary, hours, medical and retirement packages, vacation time, job risks, and several other factors when determining the attractiveness of a job. My antismoking friend couldn't work in a bar because of his asthma, so he became an accomplished scholar instead. In his case, maybe it was a good thing that the bars in Montreal never banned smoking.

Along similar lines, consider the incentives of an owner of a restaurant or bar, or any other work establishment for that matter. If you own a business, you want your employees to be productive. If you have smoking and nonsmoking employees at odds with each other, this may hurt your business. But this is a private matter. Just as a restaurant owner can try to determine the best smoking policy for customers, an employer can determine the best smoking policy for workers. This policy may involve a complete ban at the workplace, or special smoking areas, or nothing at all, but there exists a market mechanism that can deal with the issue of smoking at the work place. This market mechanism may not work perfectly, and social intervention may be useful in dealing with ETS, but the main point I am trying to make is that social intervention is not *necessarily* required to handle the negative externality of secondhand smoke in "public" places.

DOES DEATH DESERVE SOME CREDIT?

If you were to compare the medical costs incurred by a smoker and a nonsmoker, the evidence is clear that a smoker has higher medical costs. However, on average smokers live six to eight fewer years than nonsmokers. So, from a lifetime perspective, smokers may incur fewer costs involving nursing home care, pension payments, and social security payments. Let me just get this out of the way quickly: from a financial perspective, the early death of smokers may be providing a *benefit* in terms of savings on certain costs.

The concept of a financial savings, or a *death credit*, that smokers yield because of their lower life expectancy is extremely controversial. When individual states began pursuing lawsuits against the tobacco companies in the mid 1990s, the argument justifying the damages sought was a simple one: tobacco makes people ill; the states, through Medicaid, incur expenses to care for the ill; and the tobacco companies should be responsible for these expenses. But what if the overall expenses incurred by smokers fall short of the expenses incurred by nonsmokers? What, then, are the financial damages suffered by the states due to tobacco?

When the idea of a death credit was initially raised, it was greeted with such words as *ghoulish, repugnant, and immoral*. But let me recast the idea of a death credit in a way that may make it seem more plausible. Assume you are bearing the financial responsibility of caring for an elderly relative who resides in a private nursing home. There comes a time when, sadly, your relative passes away. At that point, however, the nursing home continues to bill you for six more years. It is unlikely that you are going to be willing to pay for six more years of costs that are never incurred by the nursing home. Please keep in mind that I am not claiming that you are better off because your relative passed away. You may gladly have been willing to incur six more years of expenses to take care of your relative. But there is no denying that your financial burden was eased at the passing of your relative. Does that really seem ghoulish to you?

There have been several studies that have attempted to estimate the financial costs smokers impose on society, and there has been a fair amount of disagreement as to what should be included in the analysis, and how the estimation should be conducted. I'm going to focus on one approach that has attempted to estimate the *differential* financial costs, per pack of cigarettes, between smokers and nonsmokers. For my purposes, I'd like to illustrate how the concept of a death credit can enter into this estimation, without going into the minute details of how the estimation is conducted.

If you compare the lifetime financial costs of smokers and non-smokers, what items can be included that lead to higher costs for smokers? First, there are total medical care costs. Smoking definitely adversely affects the health of smokers and leads to higher medical costs. Second, there are sick leave costs. Smokers tend to take more sick leave because of their poorer health. Third, there are group-life insurance costs. With a shorter expected life span, the inclusion of smokers in life insurance pools increases the premiums that must be paid. Fourth, smoking can lead to fires, and fire insurance costs are higher for smokers. Finally, again because of their shorter life span, smokers contribute less in earnings taxes, such as social security taxes to the government. If you add all these differential costs up, you will have a positive dollar amount, per pack of cigarettes, that indicates the excess financial costs smokers impose on society relative to non-smokers.

But what about the benefit side of the story? There are two main components in which smokers are likely to have lower financial costs than nonsmokers. First, their lower life expectancy leads to lower nursing home costs. Second, many smokers die before they reclaim money from retirement and pension plans, or they die before much is reclaimed. Nonsmokers can be more costly to finance with these types of plans. If you add these benefits together, you get the death credit, which is likely to be a negative dollar amount that indicates the excess financial *benefit* smokers impose on society relative to non-smokers.

When you put the costs and the benefits together, it is possible that they sum to a negative dollar amount. If this is the case, one could argue that smoking is, in effect, a self-financing activity. Smokers are *less* of a financial drain on society than are nonsmokers. But it could also easily be the other way around: the costs may outweigh the benefits. Both outcomes have been supported by the available evidence.

Unfortunately, there is no consensus on how to conduct this type of study. How are the dollar amounts calculated? Should excise taxes on cigarettes be considered as part of the financial benefits smokers impose on society? Should there be a broader view of costs and benefits? For example, should the studies include secondhand smoke costs or the lost value of human life? Some argue that the original lawsuits brought by individual states only considered the financial costs to the states as appropriate damages. If this is true, it may be incorrect to include broader concepts of costs and benefits. Whatever the case, it must be made clear that the cost-benefit analysis being done is either a narrow financial one, or a more encompassing societal one. Both types of analyses are legitimate, but they answer different questions.

However you feel about these types of studies, the key point I am trying to make is that the concept of a death credit is important. If it is excluded from the analysis, the net financial costs of smoking are going to be exaggerated. If it is included, there is a possibility, but not a guarantee, that cigarettes can be found to be self-financing. If one criticism is that smokers impose a financial drain on society due to excessive insurance costs, the death credit reduces the impact of that criticism.

One last point about the death credit. Recently, I was lecturing on the pros and cons of developing a market for the selling of organs for transplant. I asked my class if they could think of some benefits of developing such a market. One student quickly answered that a market would increase the supply of organs relative to what exists now. Before I could respond, another student surprised me by saying that increasing the supply of organs may be a bad thing to do. When I asked her why, she responded by saying that there is a benefit to society if people die young, just as I discussed when I lectured about smoking and the death credit. Well, at least one student was paying attention during that lecture!

I am not claiming that death is a good thing. Not at all. But tradeoffs exist everywhere, even in death. If one is trying to argue that the states are incurring an excessive financial burden by taking care of sick smokers, it is a fact that the burden is lessened when smokers die. It is also a fact that smokers die younger than nonsmokers, but not due to social intervention. Remember, smoking is a *choice*, not a requirement. You may believe that it is not a well-informed choice, or that smokers are addicted, or that other factors that I discussed in the previous chapter are at work, but no one is actually forcing smokers to smoke just so they can die young.

SEARCHING FOR THE TRUTH

As I mentioned earlier, there is a scientific debate about the health costs of environmental tobacco smoke. There are studies presenting results on both sides: some find ETS creates substantial health risks; others find that ETS poses no significant health risks. Part of the problem with these studies is that measuring the health risks of ETS can be very difficult to do.

When considering the health effects of exposure to *firsthand* smoke, one can collect data on smokers' behavior, specifically how many cigarettes they smoke and how long they've been smoking. Measuring exposure to secondhand smoke, however, is far less precise. One common approach is to compare the health risks of spouses who are married to smokers relative to spouses who are not married to smokers. To the extent that the spouses with husbands or wives who smoke have worse health outcomes, these outcomes may be attributed to exposure to secondhand smoke. But it is difficult to measure exactly how exposed a spouse is to a husband's or wife's smoke. Also, is the nonsmoking spouse exposed to ETS elsewhere, such as at work? Is the nonsmoking spouse exposed to other possible carcinogens that can be accounting for poor health outcomes? What about the lifestyle of the nonsmoking spouse in terms of diet and exercise? There are many other complicating factors, some of which can be taken into account, but some of which cannot.

The fact that the scientific evidence on the health risks of ETS is far from conclusive does not mean there are no health risks. Furthermore, there is no doubt that ETS imposes costs on individuals with breathing problems. Also, although it may sound trivial, nonsmokers may simply be bothered by the smell of smoke on their clothes or in their hair, or they may not like the smell of smoke while they are trying to eat. These types of externalities may not increase adverse health outcomes, but they are externalities nevertheless.

There is one further aspect of the empirical research on ETS that I would like to discuss. In May 2003, the *British Medical Journal* published a study that found no adverse health effect of ETS. The study was conducted by two epidemiologists, and their results drew immediate criticism from antismoking groups. The harshest criticism, however, was not about the technical merits of the study. The criticism focused on the following footnote:

> In recent years JEE [one of the authors] has received funds originating from the tobacco industry for his tobacco related epidemiological research because it has been impossible for him to obtain equivalent funds from other sources. GCK [the other author] never received funds from the tobacco industry until last year, when he conducted an epidemiological review for a law firm which has several tobacco companies as clients.

The authors were criticized for being pawns of the tobacco industry and, as a result, the critics argued that their findings should be dismissed.

I have never been impressed with this type of criticism for any empirical study. Research that is funded by outside interests can always be tainted, *regardless* of which side of the issue the results support. Many studies that find adverse health effects of ETS are funded by the World Health Organization, the National Cancer Institute, the Environmental Protection Agency, and other organizations with possible vested interests. Researchers who are funded by these groups can just as easily be criticized for being influenced by their backers. Even without outside funding, can you ever be sure of the motives behind *any* research project? Does this really matter?

As I discussed in chapter 1, the important aspects of empirical work have to do with the integrity of the data, the ability to replicate results, and the robustness of the results to different statistical approaches. There will always be sincere disagreements as to what data and statistical techniques are appropriate to use, and I believe these are the issues that can most constructively be debated.

A SMOKING SUMMARY

My personal conclusion about the smoking issue is that I believe the costs of smoking have probably been overstated, while the benefits of smoking have definitely been understated. This is true not just in the popular press and literature, but also in the academic literature. The costs of smoking from an individual perspective may be overstated for several reasons: smokers may not underestimate the risks of smoking; smokers may not be addicts (or they may be rational addicts); and smokers may not be adversely affected by cigarette advertising. The benefits of smoking are often completely ignored, yet benefits accrue to smokers, tobacco companies and their employees, retailers, and the government through the collection of cigarette tax revenue. As for the external costs smokers impose on others, the evidence on the costs of ETS is ambiguous and, compared to nonsmokers, smokers may provide a net financial savings due to their lower life expectancies.

I honestly have no idea if the costs of smoking grossly exceed the benefits, or vice versa. It may be sound social policy to reduce the consumption of cigarettes, and maybe even to completely ban them. On the other hand, it may be sound social policy to pull back on some of the current antismoking regulations. On whichever side of the debate you find yourself, I believe that a better understanding of *all* the trade-offs associated with smoking can only lead to better-informed policy decisions.

My antismoking friend once expressed his viewpoint on smoking quite simply. He supports a complete ban on smoking because he sincerely believes it is the best social solution. How could I argue against that position? I did, however, ask him to accept the premise that the best outcome is not truly known. What policy option would he choose in that case? His response was that he would err on the side of health and safety and still recommend a complete ban. I disagreed with him. My response was that I would err on the side of personal freedom and let individuals and restaurant and bar owners decide for themselves how best to deal with the smoking issue. What I didn't tell him, however, is that if he had said he would err on the side of personal freedom, I would have convincingly said that I would err on the side of health and safety. That is why I love being an economist—I'm trained to be disagreeable.

NOTES

The two sunlight cases cited and discussed are *Fontainebleau Hotel Corp. v. Forty-Five Twenty-Five Inc.*, 114 So.2d 357 (1959), and *Prah v. Maretti*, 108 Wis.2d 223 (1982).

The seminal work on social costs and property rights is by Ronald Coase, "The Problem of Social Cost," *Journal of Law and Economics* 3 (1960): 1–44. The topic of negative externalities is always well covered in any law and economics text, for example A. Mitchell Polinsky's *An Introduction to Law and Economics*, 2d ed. (Boston: Little, Brown, and Co., 1989), and Robert Cooter and Thomas Ulen's *Law and Economics*, 3d ed. (Reading, MA: Addison-Wesley, 2000).

W. Kip Viscusi offers an extensive discussion of the social costs of smoking in *Smoke-Filled Rooms* (Chicago: University of Chicago Press, 2002). He discusses environmental tobacco smoke in chapter 6, and the financial costs smokers impose on society in chapters 4 and 5.

Viscusi's work is controversial, and there are several sources that critique his approach or take a different one. For example, see Maribeth Coller, Glenn W. Harrison, and Melayne Morgan McInnes, "Evaluating the Tobacco Settlement Damage Awards: Too Much or Not Enough?" *American Journal of Public Health* 92 (2002): 1–6; David M. Cutler, et al., "How Good a Deal Was the Tobacco Settlement?: Assessing Payments to Massachusetts," *Journal of Risk and Uncertainty* 21 (2000): 235–61; and especially Jon D. Hanson and Kyle D. Logue, "The Costs of Cigarettes: The Economic Case for Ex Post Incentive-Based Regulation," *Yale Law Journal* 107 (1998): 1163–1361.

The *British Medical Journal* article that found no adverse health effect of ETS is by James E. Enstrom and Geoffrey C. Kabat, "Environmental Tobacco Smoke and Tobacco Related Mortality in a Prospective Study of Californians, 1960–98," *British Medical Journal* 326 (2003): 1057–66. Also see the editorial that precedes the article.

7 Behave Yourself

HAVE YOU ever driven a rented car? There is something so liberating about driving someone else's car, especially when you have complete insurance coverage. The parking space that might be a bit of a tight fit no longer worries you. The seventy-two-ounce super drink that doesn't fit in the beverage holder no longer distracts you. You don't have to worry about using cheap gas, squealing the tires, or slamming on the brakes. Driving a rented car is a pleasure.

You may be thinking to yourself that no responsible adult would ever abuse a rented car in those ways, at least not on purpose. You may be right, but let me restate the issue. Have you ever loaned your car to someone? What goes through your mind when you do? Do you give the driver a list of instructions to make sure they take good care of your car? Or do you just quietly worry about your car being mishandled? Do you have a slight feeling of hesitation just as you hand over the car keys? If you answered yes to these questions, you have a good idea of what I'm getting at. People tend to take better care with their own property than they would with your property. Ownership in and of itself can affect behavior. If you doubt that statement, just ask any landlord what they think, especially in a college town.

Economists have their own way of thinking about behavior in some settings. In this chapter, I'm going to present a series of short examples of some of these settings. The main point that I want to get across to you is one you often get from a *Twilight Zone* episode: *things are not always what they seem to be.*

BUCKLE UP FOR SAFETY, OR MAYBE NOT

I was home during Christmas break one year, after just completing the first half of an economics of law course. That course greatly affected the way I thought about economics. One night, at the dinner table, my father asked me how school was going. I told him that I was enjoying the law course, and he asked me about some of the topics I was studying. One recent topic involved a safety analysis of mandatory seat belt laws.

If you wear your seat belt when you drive, you feel safer. If you wear a seat belt and are in an accident, the risk of being seriously injured goes down. This feeling of security, however, may actually lead you to drive more carelessly. In effect, the costs of driving carelessly have decreased, so you drive more carelessly. My father was skeptical about this line of reasoning. He replied by saying, "You mean to tell me that when I wear my seat belt, it affects the way I drive?" I told him that's exactly what I meant.

My father wasn't buying my argument, which is a common response I get from students and others I have talked to about seat belts. It's quite reasonable to disbelieve that your driving behavior will be affected by wearing a seat belt, but it's not any single individual's behavior that matters. There may be many like my father who truly don't drive any differently when wearing a seat belt. But the argument may hold true for some drivers, and if that is the case, mandatory seat belt laws have the potential to actually *increase* the accident rate. Drivers may be relatively safer if an accident occurs, but other drivers, pedestrians, bicyclists, and motorcyclists may be less safe. This effect is known as *offsetting behavior.* The technological safety aspects of seat belts may be offset by the behavioral responses of drivers being more careless.

When I ask people who wear seat belts whether or not they drive more carelessly, and they say they don't, I like to rephrase the question: "What would you do if the next time you got into your car, the seat belt was broken and you couldn't wear it?" Often times, people respond by saying that they would drive *more* carefully until the seat belt was repaired. Doesn't that imply that they would drive *less* carefully when the seat belt was not broken?

THE SUN AND I

Have you ever been annoyed by those television commercials for local news that go something like this: "a new study finds a common household item to be deadly; tune in at eleven for all the details, along with sports and tomorrow's weather update." One day, one of those commercials caught my attention: "a new study finds that sunblock increases your chance of getting skin cancer; tune in at eleven and we'll give you the details." That worried me because I had just started wearing sunblock to *lower* my chance of getting skin cancer. It was just my luck that after years of supposedly being reckless with my health, I took a precaution that turned out to be a carcinogen.

As the day wore on, I started to think about this problem a bit more carefully. I began to seriously doubt that the sunblock I was using was, in and of itself, a carcinogen. Then I figured out what the study must be about. When people wear sunblock, they may get the feeling that they are protected from the sun for hours on end. I guessed that the study was going to demonstrate offsetting behavior: wearing sunblock was increasing individuals' exposure to the sun, negating the effect of the sunblock. When I tuned in at eleven, that is exactly what the story was about. I was, however, taken by surprise with the latest weather update. The next day was going to be hot and sunny. They recommended wearing sunblock if you were going to be outside.

HOCKEY NIGHT IN CANADA

If you grew up in Canada, the expression *Hockey Night in Canada* is well known to you. Every Saturday night during the hockey season, a hockey game was shown on television. If you lived in Montreal in the 1970s, which I did, you had the privilege of sharing your city with the greatest hockey team in the world at that time—the Montreal Canadians. Unfortunately, I was a Boston Bruins fan. The one-time coach of the Bruins, Don Cherry, made a controversial prediction back in 1979. In a recent interview, he reflected on that prediction:

In the old days, we never even thought of hitting anyone headfirst into the boards. Never! In 1979 when they put helmets on and got all protected, I predicted you would have head injuries like you wouldn't believe because guys took more liberties hitting one another. We have more concussions now in a week than we used to have in a year. (*Reader's Digest Canadian Edition,* March 2003, 64–65)

Don Cherry clearly understood the concept of offsetting behavior. If you require an athlete in a contact sport to wear more protective equipment, that will make the athlete safer only if it doesn't affect the behavior of the players. Protected players feel safer and, therefore, can be more aggressive. Also, if your rivals are more protected, you may feel that you can't hurt them as easily, so you are not as worried about hitting them. This is exactly the seat belt phenomenon applied to contact sports. It can also apply to protective equipment for skateboarding, bicycling, rollerblading, and other potentially dangerous activities. You may think you are protecting your children by making them wear protective equipment, but you may actually be increasing their chances of injury if they become more daring.

SAFE FOR CHILDREN, BUT NOT FOR ADULTS

Child poisoning is a serious problem. In the early 1970s, the Consumer Product Safety Commission (CPSC) had the extremely good intention of protecting children by enforcing child safety cap regulations, especially for common household items like aspirin. Safety caps make it difficult, but not impossible, for children to remove the caps and ingest the medicine. How can anyone argue against that regulation? Although you can debate whether or not social intervention is needed for firms to take safety precautions, I'll save that topic for chapter 8. For now, I want to consider the behavioral implications of the CPSC's safety cap regulation.

There appear to be two offsetting behavioral problems with safety cap regulation for aspirin. First, because adults feel that the safety caps are technically effective and cannot be opened by children, they may tend to leave unopened bottles in plain view. Without the safety caps, many adults may leave aspirin locked away, or at least out of plain sight. With the safety caps, there may be a tendency to leave the aspirin on a bathroom or kitchen counter. This easier access to the aspirin can lead to more child poisoning if the caps do not completely prevent child tampering. Second, safety caps can be difficult to open for some adults, especially ones who have arthritis or other pains in their hands, and this may increase the tendency for these individuals not to always replace the caps. In this case, there may be more poisonings from open bottles. Thus, offsetting behavior can work against the desired goal of the safety cap regulation. Increased safety is not solely a technical problem; it is also a problem of how people behave with technical safeguards.

A LITTLE KNOWLEDGE CAN BE A DANGEROUS THING

One of the leading weapons in the fight against the spread of H I V is information. To encourage individuals to get blood tests, one form of social intervention is to have the government subsidize the cost of the tests. The commonsense argument is that if people are aware of their H I V status, they will be able to adjust their behavior appropriately and prevent the additional spread of the disease. One interesting study, however, argues that just the opposite may happen. The authors of "The Impact of Public Testing for Human Immunodeficiency Virus" claim that information about H I V status may lead to an *increase* in the spread of the disease.

If you don't know your H I V status, a blood test will inform you if you are HIV positive or negative. How will you respond to this information? The answer depends on what you think your H I V status is *before* you take the test. For example, let's assume you are a very low risk individual and believe you are H I V negative. If the blood test confirms your belief, there is no reason to expect much change in your behavior: you're not really learning anything new. But let's say the blood test reveals that you are H I V positive. In this case, you are in a higher risk category than you thought you were. This new information may change your behavior and help reduce the spread of the disease.

Now let's assume you are a very high risk individual and believe you are HIV positive. If the blood test confirms your belief, once again there is no reason to expect much change in your behavior. But if the blood test reveals that you are HIV negative, you are actually in a lower risk category than you thought you were. In this case, the new information may change your behavior by prompting you to take more risks, and this may help spread the disease.

The authors of the study present some empirical evidence to support their claim. Using survey data from individuals who were required to have a blood test to participate in the study, they were able to determine which individuals knew their HIV status before the test (the control group), and which individuals learned their HIV status because of the test. Sexual promiscuousness was measured by comparing the number of sexual partners one year prior to the test to the number of partners one year after the test. What they found was that individuals who learned what they already believed didn't significantly change their behavior. Individuals who learned they were HIV positive when they believed they were HIV negative, did reduce their number of sexual partners. This group, however, was a very small proportion of the total sample. Individuals who learned they were HIV negative when they believed they were HIV positive, did increase their number of sexual partners. Thus, the authors concluded that it was possible that the subsidized testing for HIV may actually increase the spread of the disease.

Although it is just a single study, and the empirical evidence is far from definitive, I believe the main point of the study has nothing to do with the empirical results. The commonsense belief that more HIV testing will help reduce the spread of the disease may not be accurate. At least the theoretical possibility exists that offsetting behavior may lead to results that are totally at odds with the intention of subsidized blood tests.

The tricky role of the behavioral response to new information in terms of social policy was also discussed in chapter 5 with respect to smoking. If smokers tend to overestimate the risks of smoking, they may be smoking less than they would if they were perfectly informed. With the HIV study, individuals who believe they are in a high risk category may be less sexually promiscuous than they would be if they were perfectly informed. Is it sound social policy to provide accurate information if that can lead to an *increase* in risky behavior? That is a difficult question to answer, but understanding the role of behavioral responses to social policy can help lead to more informed policy.

HAZARDOUS TO YOUR MORALS

Most people have some form of insurance for something or other. You may insure your health, car, home, property, and other things that are valuable to you. Insurance allows you to pay a premium to cover a potential loss that can substantially outweigh the premium. For example, you buy car insurance for $500 a year. If at the end of the year you had the good fortune not to have an accident and make a claim, you don't get your $500 refunded. But if you were in an accident, your insurance company would pay for damages that could be in the thousands of dollars. Insurance companies can survive because they keep all the premiums paid to them, and only pay out when accidents occur. The premiums, then, are largely determined by the probabilities that accidents occur and by the amount of losses that the insurance companies have to pay out. (Premiums also depend on the costs of operating an insurance company, but this won't be of primary importance for what I want to discuss.)

Let's say that included as part of the coverage for your $500 car insurance premium is theft coverage. If your car is stolen, your insurance company will reimburse you the *full* current value of your car. In other words, if your car is stolen and you have insurance, in a sense you still own the same car. The probability that your car is stolen can depend on many things—where you live, whether or not you park in a garage, the type of car you drive, and so on. Insurance companies spend a great deal of time determining these types of probabilities because they are an integral part of setting premiums. However, one complication that insurance companies face is that the selling of insurance in and of itself may affect the probability of a loss occurring.

An insurance company pays attention to many things when you buy insurance. Where you live and what type of car you drive are two of them. Whether or not you park in a garage, however, may not be one of them. If not, the insurance company may face a problem known as *moral hazard*. Assume that you can lower the probability of your car being stolen if you park it in a garage. The sensible thing to do, then, may be to park in a garage. But parking in a garage may be costly to you, either because of the parking fee you may have to pay, or even because of the bother of getting into and out of a garage. If you are fully covered for the loss of your car in case of theft, what benefit would you get from parking in a garage? If the car is stolen, you will be fully compensated. So, for some positive cost of protecting your car, you receive no additional benefit. The full insurance, in effect, alters your incentive to take care of your car. This is the moral hazard problem: the insurance coverage changes the way you behave and increases the probability of your car being stolen.

There are two key factors behind moral hazard. The first involves an unobservable action. If the insurance company can observe all actions that affect the probability of an accident, your insurance premium can be adjusted to reflect your behavior. The more care you take to lower the probability of an accident, the lower will be your premium. If your insurance company requires you to park in a garage to be compensated for a loss, there will be no moral hazard problem. You may decide not to buy theft insurance if you feel parking in a garage is an unreasonable condition, or you may have to buy insurance at a higher premium. But if you insure, your premium will depend on your actions.

The second important factor behind moral hazard is the concept of full insurance. Even if the insurance company fully compensates you for the value of your car, are you really *fully* insured if your car is stolen? There will be other costs you incur that are not insurable, such as your time costs of dealing with the loss, your frustration, the inconvenience of having to find substitute transportation, the bother of buying a new car, and so forth. To the extent that you have to bear part of the risk of your car being stolen, the moral hazard problem will be mitigated.

Along the same lines, insurance companies are well aware of the moral hazard problem. Quite often, insurance is not meant to provide full coverage. Deductibles are one way to allow the person buying insurance to bear some risk. Coinsurance (or partial coverage) is another way. If an insurance company is dealing with an unobservable action like keeping the car in a garage, but they realize the individual is not purchasing full coverage, that may be enough information to satisfy the insurance company that the action will be taken after all. As long as the individual is bearing enough risk to affect behavior, an unobservable action may still be taken.

Moral hazard has the potential to affect all types of insurance. One common criticism of socialized health insurance is that medical resources will be wasted because of the moral hazard problem. People who don't bear the direct risk of their actions may not take appropriate care of their health. Obviously, not everyone is going to purposely allow their health to degenerate because they have full health insurance. But on the margin, there may be some people who worry less about the risks of smoking or drinking, or about the benefits of diet and exercise.

There has been some empirical evidence to suggest that socialized medicine does have to contend with moral hazard problems, but it appears that the bulk of the evidence has not been very compelling. When it comes to health, individuals are rarely fully insured. Bad health outcomes create losses that often well exceed the insurable medical costs or lost wages. Pain and suffering costs, if not compensated, provide strong incentives for individuals to avoid moral hazard problems. Still, full insurance always raises the possibility of an increased accident rate, and moral hazard is an important factor to consider when discussing any social policy issue that involves an insurance component.

DOCTORS ON THE DEFENSE

Nobody likes to think about doctors behaving badly, but there has been a growing concern that the pressures of medical malpractice liability has led to adverse behavioral responses from doctors. Tort liability will be the subject of the next chapter, but this example concerning medical malpractice liability will provide a nice link between behavioral issues and tort law.

The concept I would like to address here is known as *defensive medicine,* and it is well defined in a 1994 Office of Technology Assessment (U.S. Congress) study:

Defensive medicine occurs when doctors order tests, procedures, or visits, or avoid high-risk patients or procedures, primarily (but not necessarily solely) to reduce their exposure to malpractice liability. When physicians do extra tests or procedures primarily to reduce malpractice liability, they are practicing positive defensive medicine. When they avoid certain patients or procedures, they are practicing negative defensive medicine.

It doesn't seem like a doctor could ever take *too much* care with their patients, but that is exactly what positive defensive medicine is concerned with. If the costs of extra medical resources outweigh the health benefits those resources lead to, too much care is being provided. With negative defensive medicine, too little care is being provided. In other words, procedures with benefits that outweigh their costs are not being provided. The key question, then, from an economic perspective is this: What is the *optimal* amount of medical care (in any given situation)? A real world legal case provides an example of how this question may be answered.

In 1959, a twenty-three-year-old woman visited her ophthalmologist, was diagnosed with nearsightedness, and was fitted with contact lenses. Through 1968, she routinely complained of eye irritation. Finally, in 1968, at the age of thirty-two, she was given an eye pressure test that indicated she had glaucoma. By that time, she had suffered severe and permanent eye damage. The court had to address the question of whether or not the doctor's initial lack of early detection of glaucoma could be deemed malpractice.

At the time, it was standard practice in ophthalmology not to apply the pressure test for anyone under the age of forty. Although two lower courts ruled in favor of the doctor, the Supreme Court of Washington state reversed the lower courts' decisions. Simply put, the Supreme Court believed that the benefit of applying the pressure test outweighed the small cost of the test:

Under the facts of this case reasonable prudence required the timely giving of the pressure test to this plaintiff. The precaution of giving this test to detect the incidence of glaucoma to patients under 40 years of age is so imperative that irrespective of its disregard by the standards of the ophthalmology profession, it is the duty of the courts to say what is required to protect patients under 40 from the damaging results of glaucoma.

Although the court believed it was optimal to apply the pressure test as part of a routine eye exam regardless of the age of the patient, it may not have been optimal from a medical standpoint. At the time of the court's decision, an expert in the field of ophthalmology reached the opposite conclusion. He argued that the incidence of glaucoma was too low and it would be an inefficient use of resources to make population screening the norm. If it is the case that it is not optimal to routinely apply the pressure test, the court's ruling could lead to the practice of defensive medicine. It may be far better for doctors to apply the test rather than face the possibility of substantial malpractice liability.

The practice of defensive medicine suggests that doctors may be inefficiently responding to the pressure of malpractice liability. Empirically, this can be a very difficult concept to verify or refute. Doctors may have many valid medical reasons for providing what may seem to be excessive care or inadequate care, and not solely as a response to malpractice liability. Two related studies by the same researchers shed some light on these issues.

In the first study, the authors look at cesarean-section delivery rates and infant health. A cesarean-section is a fairly costly surgical procedure (relative to nonsurgical deliveries) that is generally best used when complications arise. If doctors are concerned about excessive malpractice liability in delivering babies that suffer adverse health outcomes, they may practice positive defensive medicine in using a delivery method that is more costly but provides less of a risk of a bad health outcome to the baby. And although it seems that it may always be a good idea to minimize the risk to the baby, as with any other bad outcome I have discussed in this book, there are trade-offs. A cesarean-section definitely has costs that may not be offset by its benefits, especially for what would be a normal delivery without the cesarean-section.

The authors investigate whether increased malpractice liability risk is associated with more cesarean-sections but not better infant health outcomes. That would imply the costs of the increased cesarean-sections have no offsetting health benefits, which suggests evidence of positive defensive medicine. If the increased rate of cesarean-sections leads to better infant health outcomes, this makes the finding of positive defensive medicine less likely. One of the authors' conclusions is that they do find evidence of positive defensive medicine.

In another study, the authors focus on the issue of negative defensive medicine in prenatal infant health care. They argue that fear of malpractice liability may delay prenatal care, thus implying the practice of negative defensive medicine. And if this delay leads to poorer infant health outcomes, it may be efficient to begin prenatal care at an earlier stage. In this case, the authors do find that while increased malpractice liability pressure does slightly delay prenatal care, it doesn't seem to have any effect on infant health outcomes. This suggests that there may be no evidence of negative defensive medicine in this particular setting.

What the medical malpractice and other examples in this chapter demonstrate is that behavioral responses to rules and regulations may lead to significant offsetting effects that undermine the policy makers' original objectives. Social policies with excellent intentions such as mandatory seat-belt laws and child safety cap regulations require more than just a consideration of the technical aspects of the safety features to determine their effectiveness in reducing injuries. In evaluating such policies, then, a fundamental premise of economic analysis should be kept in mind: as individuals encounter changes in the trade-offs they face, their behavior will be affected.

NOTES

The seminal work on seat belt laws and offsetting behavior is by Sam Peltzman, "The Effects of Automobile Safety Regulation," *Journal of Political Economy* 83 (1975): 677–725. A more comprehensive discussion can be found in a book by Glenn Blomquist, *The Regulation of Motor Vehicle and Traffic Safety* (Boston: Kluwer Academic Publishers, 1988).

W. Kip Viscusi provides several sources on the topic of behavioral responses to safety regulation. Two good books to start with are *Fatal Tradeoffs: Public and Private Responsibili-*

ties for Risk (New York: Oxford University Press, 1992), and *Rational Risk Policy* (Oxford: Oxford University Press, 1998).

The HIV testing study is by Michael A. Boozer and Tomas J. Philipson, "The Impact of Public Testing for Human Immunodeficiency Virus," *Journal of Human Resources* 35 (2000): 419–46.

There are several chapters in Anthony J. Culyer and Joseph P. Newhouse, eds., *Handbook of Health Economics* (Amsterdam: Elsevier, 2000) that deal with insurance topics including moral hazard. You can also find this material in any health economics textbook, such as the text by Charles E. Phelps, *Health Economics,* 3d ed. (Boston: Addison-Wesley, 2003).

The U.S. Congress, Office of Technology Assessment study is titled "Defensive Medicine and Medical Malpractice," OTA-H-602, July 1994.

The ophthalmologist malpractice case is *Helling v. Carey*, 83 Wash. 2d 514 (1974). For more on medical malpractice, see the text by Werner Z. Hirsch, *Law and Economics: An Introductory Analysis,* 2d ed. (Boston: Academic Press, 1988), chapter 7.

The studies on defensive medicine and infant health care are both by Lisa Dubay, Robert Kaestner, and Timothy Waidmann, "The Impact of Malpractice Fears on Cesarean Section Rates," *Journal of Health Economics* 18 (1999): 491–522, and "Medical Malpractice Liability and Its Effect on Prenatal Care Utilization and Infant Health," *Journal of Health Economics* 20 (2001): 591–611.

8 *Warning: Beware of Products*

IMAGINE THAT you are sitting down to your favorite breakfast of toast and raspberry preserves. After spreading the preserves on your toast, you take your first mouthwatering bite. While chewing, your teeth come into contact with a gummy substance, about the size of a half dollar. You remove the substance, rinse it off under the tap, and discover that it is a mouse part. You respond immediately by vomiting, and then you feel sick for several days and cannot go to work. Furthermore, your love of raspberry preserves is lost forever. Your illness, however, doesn't prevent you from suing the manufacturer of the raspberry preserves. Your hope is that the manufacturer will be held liable for your damages, and you feel confident that you will prevail. After all, a mouse part in a jar of raspberry preserves obviously is not part of the intended product design. How could you not prevail?

Whether or not you actually prevail depends on the tort law rule that the court will use to determine the extent of the manufacturer's liability. Tort law is the body of law that deals with wrongful acts in which private citizens can sue their injurers for damages in civil court. Automobile accidents, medical malpractice, and products liability are all common examples of activities that fall under the scope of tort law. In this chapter, I will focus exclusively on the setting of products liability, and offer just a brief introduction to this extremely broad topic in the law.

From a policy perspective, the key question in product liability law is this: What legal rule should be adopted to determine a firm's

liability in a product-related accident? There are several potential liability rules, from holding firms liable for every product-related accident, to never holding firms liable regardless of the circumstances.
Every liability rule has its staunch supporters. But, as is always the case,
the desirability of any individual rule will depend on the objective you
have in using the rule. The foremost economic objective I will focus on
is to determine how each liability rule affects a firm's behavior in choosing its safety effort (or care level) in producing its products. The cost of
increased care can be weighed against the benefit of a lowered probability of a product-related accident. I hope this doesn't leave a bad taste
in your mouth, but the implication of cost-benefit analysis in this setting is that it may be economically efficient for a mouse part to show up
in your raspberry preserves.

NOT BY DESIGN

There are several specific issues that come under the scrutiny of products
liability law, but the one I will focus on here involves what is referred to
as a *manufacturing defect*. A mouse part in the raspberry preserves is a
manufacturing defect because it is an unintended flaw due to some
mishap in the production process. In contrast, a *design defect* is considered to be a flaw that is common to every unit produced. To clearly illustrate the difference between the two types of defects, I will return to a case
I discussed in chapter 2—the Ford Pinto case.

In the Pinto case, at issue was whether or not Ford's decision not to
include the $11 safety feature in the car's design was a design defect. As
I previously discussed, the concept of optimal design requires a consideration of the costs and benefits of every possible safety feature that
can be included. The fact that the Pinto did not include the $11 feature
does not, in and of itself, tell us that there was a design defect. Instead,
we would have to compare the safety benefits of adding the feature to
the costs of adding the feature. If it was determined that the social benefits exceeded the social costs, only then would the design without the
safety feature be deemed defective.

Now, let's change the Pinto story in a way that will allow me to make
a clear distinction between a design defect and a manufacturing defect.

Assume that the Pinto *was* designed to include the $11 safety feature, but the particular Pinto that the girls were driving the day of their tragic accident did not have the safety feature in place. Due to some flaw in the manufacturing process, the safety feature was not properly placed in that particular car, which makes it a clear case of a manufacturing defect. Does the manufacturing defect, in and of itself, suggest that holding the firm liable for any product-related damages is the correct solution? When asked this question, most of my students answer "yes." Their reasoning usually involves the belief that the defect speaks for itself. The question I want to raise is this: If the defect speaks for itself, exactly what is the defect saying?

In any manufacturing process, there is always a chance that a product will be produced defectively, that is, not as it was designed to be produced. Using a hypothetical example, assume that a firm produces one million units of a product, and the probability of a manufacturing defect is two in one million. Thus, *on average*, the firm can expect to produce two defective units. (Notice that the *exact* number of defective units may not be two, as the manufacturing defect only occurs with some probability.) If each defective unit leads to a damage of $100, the total *expected damages* caused by the defect will be $200.

Let's assume that the firm can spend $75 to increase its safety effort and reduce the probability of a defect to one in one million. Thus, for $75 the firm can lower the expected number of defects from two units to one unit, and lower the expected damages by $100. From a cost-benefit perspective, the cost of lowering the defect rate is $75, but the benefit in terms of reduced damages is $100. The socially efficient outcome, then, is for the firm to reduce the defect rate. That is, from an economic standpoint, the initial defect rate of two in one million is *not* efficient.

To provide an incentive for the firm to take the efficient level of safety precaution, tort law establishes a liability rule that determines the extent of liability the firm faces when a consumer suffers damages from a defective unit. One such rule is *strict liability*, which holds a firm liable for damages for every product-related accident independent of how much care the firm was taking in terms of safety. Under a rule of strict liability, if the firm does not increase its safety effort it is liable for expected damages of $200. If it does increase its safety effort, it is liable for only $100. Thus, by spending $75, the firm lowers its expected liability by $100. It is clearly in the firm's best interest to reduce the defect rate to one in one million, and this perfectly matches the efficient outcome.

Now let's assume that the firm can further lower the defect rate from one in one million to zero, thus reducing the expected damage by another $100. The cost of this increased safety effort, however, is $150. From an economic standpoint, it is not worth spending $150 to reduce the expected damage by only $100. But will the firm take the added safety precaution if it is strictly liable for damages? The answer is no. Once at the one in one million defect rate, the firm expects to be liable for one defect leading to $100 in damages. To take the added safety precaution, the firm must spend $150. In this case, the firm prefers to pay the tort damages rather than the safety costs and will not find it in its best interest to reduce the defect rate to zero. (I am assuming that there are no legal costs the firm incurs. If there are legal costs, the firm may prefer to spend the additional $150 to save the $100 tort damages, *and* the additional legal costs.)

In this setting, strict liability is an efficient liability rule. It provides the firm with the incentive to reduce the defect rate when it is efficient to do so, and not to reduce the defect rate when that is efficient. The firm, in effect, is forced to make a private decision that is perfectly matched to the correct social decision: the firm must trade-off the costs of additional safety with the benefits of additional safety. But notice that with this reasoning, the goal of reducing the defect rate to zero is not cost efficient. It is optimal for there to be a one in one million defect rate.

Another advantage of a strict liability rule is that there is a lot of common sense associated with it. With a manufacturing defect, a product is, by definition, not produced in the way that it is designed to be produced. Why shouldn't a firm be held liable for damages in this case? It is quite likely that this commonsense argument is at least partly the reason why in real world manufacturing defect cases, strict liability is generally the rule that is used. Yet critics of strict liability do point to some serious problems with it.

Probably the most common and most critical compliant about strict liability is that it leads to a tremendous amount of litigation. Strict liability can lead to a large number of claims filed against firms. Anyone who has suffered a product-related damage is likely to have a valid claim. Legal claims, and eventual trials if warranted, are very costly to pursue. And even if these costs are privately incurred by the opposing parties, it is legitimate to question whether or not there are other liability rules that can lead to cost efficient safety efforts *without* the added burden of costly litigation.

A second criticism of strict liability involves the role of the consumer in affecting the probability of a product-related accident occurring. Under strict liability, a firm is liable for damages if its product has a manufacturing defect, regardless of how much safety effort the firm *or* the consumer undertook. For example, before spreading the raspberry preserves on your toast, was it possible that had you taken a quick look, you would have noticed a foreign substance before chewing the mouse part? Obviously, there are many manufacturing defects that are unlikely to ever be detected by the consumer, but this will not be true for all defects. As discussed with insurance and moral hazard in the previous chapter, if the consumer is always *fully* compensated for damages, there is no benefit to undertaking any safety effort. And even if the consumer is not fully compensated, the argument goes, strict liability can still dampen the incentive for the consumer to take care, leading to an increase in the number of product-related accidents.

These shortcomings of the strict liability rule have led many scholars to question whether or not there is an alternative liability rule that retains the advantages of strict liability, yet eliminates its disadvantages. There is such a rule, and it is known as the *negligence* rule. Unfortunately, this rule introduces its own unique set of problems.

EXCUSE MY DEFECT

Under a negligence rule, a firm can escape liability for a manufacturing defect if the firm is found to have taken a sufficient level of care, often referred to as efficient or *due* care. Consider the numerical example I introduced above. Starting with the two in one million defect rate, we know that the firm can spend $75 to reduce the defect rate to one in one million, thus saving $100. The due care defect rate, then, cannot be two in one million. To further reduce the defect rate to zero, the firm can spend $150 but save only $100 in damages. Thus, the due care rate also cannot be zero. In this example, as long as the firm can maintain a defect rate of no more than one in one million, the firm would not be found liable for any defective unit that is purchased.

From the firm's perspective, it is in its best interest to reduce the defect rate from two in one million to one in one million. For $75, not only does the firm save $100 by reducing the expected number of defective units from two to one, it also is not liable for the remaining defective unit that will be produced. The key, then, to thinking about manufacturing defects and the negligence rule is not to equate the word *defect* with the word *negligent*. A defect can exist without the firm being negligent, as long as the firm is maintaining the efficient defect rate.

Both the negligence rule and strict liability in our example provide the firm with the incentive to take due care. With strict liability, the firm cannot escape liability at the one in one million defect rate, but it is not in its best interest to spend $150 to reduce the defect rate to zero to save only $100 in expected liability. With negligence, the firm takes due care to completely avoid liability. But one of the main advantages of the negligence rule over strict liability is that under negligence, there are likely to be fewer legal claims. With negligence, a successful claim can only be made against a firm that was taking less than due care. In theory, if the negligence rule always provides the incentive for the firm to take due care, there should never be a successful claim against the firm. In practice, however, the negligence rule can be very difficult for the courts to apply.

To use strict liability, the court must determine that an accident occurred and that the accident was caused by the product. The court does not have to evaluate the level of safety effort the firm was undertaking. To use the negligence rule, the court must address two additional questions: What is the due care level of the firm, and how much *actual* care was the firm taking? These can be two very difficult questions to answer, especially with respect to manufacturing defects. Even if the court can gather evidence on the actual defect rate by observing defective units that have been produced, it then must compare the actual defect rate to the due care rate. How can the due care rate be determined? A typical manufacturing process is likely to involve numerous technological considerations, many of which may be well beyond the scope of a judge or jury to completely understand, even with the aid of expert witnesses. Thus, strict liability may be a more costly rule in terms of litigation costs, but the negligence rule is a more costly rule to apply when a claim is made. And to the extent that there are errors made in the application of the negligence rule, it may no longer provide the incentive for the firm to take due care.

Because due care levels are likely to change over time with technological developments, one argument in favor of strict liability is that it provides the firm with the incentive to continually adopt new safety efforts. Because the firm can never avoid liability, it has the incentive to constantly reevaluate its production process to adopt new cost-efficient technology. According to the negligence rule, the courts must constantly revise the meaning of due care, which will be a slow and difficult process. In this case, the firm may not have the incentive to improve its safety effort until it believes the courts will hold it negligent for a manufacturing defect.

Negligence does offer an advantage over strict liability in terms of the consumer's behavior in affecting the probability of a product-related accident. To the extent that a firm takes due care, under negligence a legal claim is less likely to be filed, or it is less likely to be successful. If the firm can avoid liability, the burden is placed on the consumer to bear damages, and the moral hazard problem is circumvented. This is often thought of as one of the great advantages of the negligence rule: not only does it provide the firm with the incentive to take efficient safety efforts, it simultaneously provides the consumer with the exact same incentive. The firm takes due care to avoid liability, and the consumer takes due care to efficiently trade-off between safety costs and safety benefits. This is assuming, of course, that the rule can be applied correctly, which is the biggest drawback of using the negligence rule.

While I am on the subject of possible consumer misuse of a product, I'd like to briefly discuss an interesting doctrine in products liability law known as *foreseeable misuse*. With this doctrine, a firm may be held liable for damages in a product-related accident even if the accident blatantly appeared to be the fault of the consumer. As an example, consider the facts of the following case. An eleven-year-old boy, while at a commercial recreational facility, tried to get change out of a two-hundred-pound change-making machine by rocking the machine back and forth. The machine tipped over onto the boy and he suffered a broken leg. The first time I ever presented the facts of this case to a class, I was surprised by their response. Almost unanimously, the class thought the eleven-year-old boy got what he deserved. One student sarcastically asked me if the boy's actions could be explained by an economic theory of stupidity! It was to this student I addressed the following question: What if the owner of the recreation facility could have spent a few dollars on a couple of metal brackets and some screws, and easily secure the machine to the wall so it couldn't be tipped over? The student immediately understood my point, and he will have to look elsewhere for a good economic theory of stupidity.

Although at first blush it sounds wrong to hold a firm liable for a product-related accident due to consumer misuse, from an economic perspective it may still be that the firm is in the best position to efficiently reduce the probability of an accident occurring. Not securing the change machine to the wall may be a perfect example of negligence on the part of the firm. Actually, that is exactly what the court ruled. But the doctrine of foreseeable misuse is not always applied successfully against a firm. When I lived in Texas, there was a story in the local newspaper about a young teenage boy and a power line. The boy took four or five tent poles and connected them together. He then used them to repeatedly hit a power line, and he ended up losing both of his arms. Could the power company have foreseen such misuse? And even had they been able to foresee such misuse, could they reasonably have done anything to prevent such an accident? The court didn't believe so, and the case was dismissed.

In this section, I have outlined some of the economic issues debated by scholars over the choice of liability rules to adopt in manufacturing defect cases. Those in favor of strict liability emphasize the strengths of that rule—it can provide the firm with the incentive to take due care, and it is a simple rule to understand and apply. Those in favor of the negligence rule highlight its strengths—it can provide the incentive for the firm *and* the consumer to take due care, and it reduces the number of legal claims that are made. As the relative merits of each rule may be debated forever, some economists favor an alternative approach to products liability: a rule of *no* liability at all.

IS THE ONLY GOOD LIABILITY RULE
A NO LIABILITY RULE?

Let me ask you a "how comfortable are you with the following idea" question: On a scale from 0 to 10, with 0 being the least comfortable and 10 being the most comfortable, how comfortable would you be living in a society in which firms faced absolutely no products liability law at all—a world of complete *caveat emptor?* The most common answer I get from my students is 0. It just doesn't sound right to most people that firms would be adequately concerned with producing safe products if there were no laws that forced them to be concerned. If you were to ask professional economists the same question, however, I assure you that you would get some sincere answers of 10. Does that make you feel more comfortable?

How a rule of no liability can provide the incentive for a firm to take due care is related to two concepts I discussed in earlier chapters—*full price* and *gains from trade.* When I discussed the risks associated with smoking, I argued that the full price of a pack of cigarettes is primarily made up of two components: the dollar amount that you have to pay, and a nonmonetary amount that reflects any potential risks you must bear. Under a rule of no liability, the consumer bears all product-related risks, so the full price the consumer pays typically exceeds the monetary price. To maximize gains from trade, then, the consumer is interested in paying the lowest full price for a product, *not* necessarily the lowest monetary price.

For example, assume you are considering buying an automatic garage door opener. There are two models to choose from that are identical except for one feature: the more expensive model includes a safety feature that prevents the door from lowering when anything is beneath it. The model without the safety feature costs $1000, and the model with the feature costs $1200. If the firm is not liable for any garage door related accident, and you don't purchase the model with the safety feature, your *expected damages* are $300. In other words, if you face a 5% chance of suffering damages of $6000, *on average* your damages are (5%)($6000), or $300. With the safety feature, your expected damages are zero. From your perspective, the full price of the garage door without the safety feature is $1300, that is, a $1000 monetary price and $300 in expected damages. But with the safety feature, your full price is only $1200. Thus, you pay a lower full price and receive an additional $100 in gains from trade if you purchase the model with the safety feature.

The main point is that if consumers have perfect information about the product risks they face, a firm has the incentive to take due care *independent* of the liability rules, including the rule of no liability. This is a powerful market result because it suggests that due care in terms of product safety can be achieved without incurring any of the administration costs of the tort system. Firms can compete against each other to provide safety features that consumers demand, and the firms that can maintain the lowest *full* prices will be the most successful. But even when considering firms that enjoy some monopoly power, they too have an incentive to provide safety features when there are gains from trade to be exploited. Safety can be thought of as a product, just like any other product, and market forces can encourage its provision. But before we dismantle the products liability legal system, we may want to ask an important question: What if consumers *misperceive* the risks they face?

If consumers are not aware, or typically underestimate, the product risks they face, a rule of no liability is unlikely to provide the correct incentive for firms to take due care with safety features. With the garage door example, if you incorrectly believe there is no product risk without the safety feature, the less expensive model will also appear to have the lower full price. The monetary price of $1000 is the full price, at least as far as you are concerned, so you would not want to purchase the $1200 model with the safety feature. Liability rules, in this case, may have some bite.

With strict liability, the firm is liable for product-related damages regardless of the consumer's perception of product risk. The garage door manufacturer will avoid the expected damage of $300 by including the safety feature that costs less than $300. Under the negligence rule, the firm must adhere to the court's definition of due care to avoid liability, again regardless of the consumer's perception of risk. If the court concludes that due care is the garage door model with the safety feature, it will be in the firm's best interest to add a safety feature that costs less than $300.

While there is much debate over which liability rule is best, there tends to be a wide agreement that at least *some* rule is needed, especially to overcome consumers' lack of perfect information of the risks they face. But even if a rule of no liability has its shortcomings in the real world, no one can argue that it doesn't have tremendous benefits in terms of eliminating litigation costs. So, maybe what is needed is a way to preserve the benefits of a rule of no liability and, at the same time, reduce its shortcomings.

YOU'VE BEEN WARNED

If good product-risk information is needed to allow a market mechanism to provide the firm the incentive to take due care, maybe firms should be encouraged to provide warnings with their products. If product warnings allow consumers to make well-informed decisions, liability rules may not be needed to encourage firms to make efficient safety decisions. But then we are faced with a key question: How do we encourage firms to provide optimal warnings? Furthermore, what is an optimal warning?

Recently, I purchased a set of cooking knives. The packaging contained the following warning:

> Use caution when handling cutlery. As with all sharp objects, keep out of reach of children. Never try to catch falling cutlery or test blade sharpness with fingers. Mishandling of cutlery may result in injury.

How useful is that warning to you? Will it affect your behavior when dealing with sharp knives? If you do cut yourself with a sharp knife that *doesn't* provide a similar warning, does that suggest you should have a successful legal claim against the knife company?

In *warning defect* cases, the courts must identify an optimal warning, and then place liability on a firm that does not provide that warning. Thus, a warning defect case is very similar to a design defect case in that the word *defect* implies negligence. The concept of an optimal warning is tricky business. A warning shouldn't be too general, such as, *warning: this product is dangerous.* A warning also shouldn't be too technically complicated. Furthermore, there have been studies that suggest too much information may dilute the important aspects of the warning or tire consumers, discouraging them from completely reading or understanding the warning. If liability for a warning defect provides the incentive for the firm to provide perfect information to the consumer, it is possible that market incentives can provide the firm with the incentive to take due care in terms of safety, even without any further liability rules being used.

One of the most interesting aspects of warning defect cases involves warnings that fail to inform of a risk because that risk was not known at the time. For example, a woman developed discolored teeth as a result of a drug she had taken since she was a child. The drug controlled upper respiratory and other types of infections. It was effective as an antibiotic, but the drug company did not warn physicians of the side effect of teeth discoloration. One of the defenses of the drug company was that they simply did not know of the tooth discoloration problem at the time their product was initially marketed. Although one can argue that it is unreasonable to a hold a firm liable for failing to warn about a risk that they did not know about, the relevant issue becomes whether or not the firm *could* have known about the risk.

If a risk can be ascertained through undertaking a certain amount of research, an optimal warning would include that risk if the cost of research is less than the benefit of warning about that risk. Had the drug company been able to undertake a simple study that quickly determined the side effect of the drug, it likely would have been negligent in failing to undertake that study. If, however, the discoloration problem would have taken decades to reveal itself, thus possibly delaying the marketing of a valuable drug for many years, the firm likely would not be considered negligent for failing to warn of the risk. It is possible, however, that a firm is dealing with a risk that is truly unknowable at the time. If no amount of research could possibly reveal the risk, the optimal warning could not include that risk.

TO TORT OR NOT TO TORT

No matter how you weigh the relative merits of the different liability rules, the most common discussed shortcoming of the tort system is its administration costs. Every rule other than no liability can be substantially costly to implement, either due to the costs of filing legal claims or to the costs of implementing the rules. These costs have lead scholars to consider alternative systems for providing safety incentives to firms and consumers.

One alternative to tort law for product-related accidents is to adopt contract law instead. Under a rule of no liability, if consumers still value some implicit liability rule, firms can offer legally binding warranties. Purchasing a warranty can be thought of in exactly the same way as purchasing a product. If there are gains from trade in selling a warranty, both parties will benefit from the transaction.

Warranties, however, may not add much to a rule of no liability in terms of safety incentives. As discussed above, if consumers have perfect information, no liability provides the correct incentive for firms to take due care. It is only with imperfect information that no liability can be an inefficient rule because consumers may misperceive the risks they face and not correctly value additional safety features. The key issue, then, is how warranties can help alleviate the problem of risk misperception.

If consumers are not well-informed about product risks, the warranties they desire may be too broad or too narrow compared to the optimal warranties. But one advantage of warranties is that they can vary from consumer to consumer. Different consumers undoubtedly place different values on product warranties, especially since product risks are likely to vary across consumer groups. Warranties can be tailored to individual consumers. For example, in many electronic or appliance stores, customers are routinely offered an additional service contract at an additional charge. Consumers who place little value on these extended warranties simply can refuse to purchase them.

One final note about warranties. Although contract law may involve fewer administration costs than tort law, it still can be very costly to use. Breach of contract cases can be complicated. And even if the contract has specific damage remedies clearly laid out, it is not uncommon for courts to circumvent these agreed-upon remedies. This makes exploiting the gains from trade from contracting difficult to do. If you are trying to negotiate a contract, but realize that later the terms of the contract may be deemed void, this will reduce the value of contracting in the first place. Still, many economists favor the contract solution because it does place the issue of product safety into the hands of the private parties involved in the transaction.

Another alternative to tort law is government regulation of product safety. I have discussed government intervention several times throughout the book, so I will be brief here. A strong economic justification for government intervention is when a market failure exists and the regulation can mimic what the market solution would likely have been. This, of course, can be very difficult to do. Not only does the regulating body have to determine the appropriate safety standards for firms to follow, they must be able to monitor and enforce the standards, as well as punish violators. Consumer complaints will certainly aid in the enforcement of the regulations, but how government intervention compares to tort or contract law in providing incentives for due care and in administration costs is an open question.

In my opinion, the most important point to consider in comparing tort law, contract law, and government regulation, is to recognize that all three of these options are not only substitutes for each other in some dimensions, but also complements to each other in other dimensions. The optimal way to confront the trade-offs associated with product safety is to determine how best the three systems can work together. This likely isn't the case right now. For example, consider a design defect case. If there is a government design standard that is in place, a firm that falls short of that standard is almost certainly going to be found negligent in a tort case. But if it is shown that the firm has met or exceeded that standard, the firm may still be found negligent. A negligence rule is difficult to apply, and it may be efficient to peg due care to a regulatory standard to minimize the information costs of using that rule. It is certainly worth considering how the different systems interact with each other.

NOTES

Two excellent sources on the economics of tort law that have influenced me greatly are by William M. Landes and Richard A. Posner, *The Economic Structure of Tort Law* (Cambridge, MA: Harvard University Press, 1987), and Steven Shavell, *Economic Analysis of Accident Law* (Cambridge, MA: Harvard University Press, 1987). Another interesting source specifically on products liability law is by W. Kip Viscusi, *Reforming Products Liability* (Cambridge, MA: Harvard University Press, 1991).

The citation for the actual case about the mouse part in the raspberry preserves is *Young v. Great Atlantic & Pacific Tea Co.*, 15 F. Supp. 1018 (1936).

The case about the boy and the change-making machine is *Ridenour v. Bat Em Out*, 707 A. 2d 1093 (1998).

The case about the drug and discolored teeth is *Feldman v. Lederle Laboratories*, 479 A. 2d 374 (1984).

For a discussion of the advantages of contract law over tort law, see Paul H. Rubin, *Tort Reform by Contract* (Washington, D.C.: AEI Press, 1993).

9 *There Are No Solutions*

WHERE WERE you when the lights went out on the East Coast and throughout parts of the Midwest on August 14, 2003? I was fortunate not to lose power, so I was able to watch some of the news coverage of the situation. Most of the early news stories focused on the human interest aspects of the blackout—people stuck in subways, tourists sleeping on the sidewalks, thousands of pedestrians walking home—and on trying to identify what caused the problem. Before too long, however, the experts were called in to discuss the solution to the problem, even before anyone precisely knew what the problem was.

There were basically two broad categories of solutions. The first was that the blackout was due to government regulation of the electric power industry. The industry needed to be deregulated so that the power companies could earn sufficient profit allowing them to invest in better technology. The second category also agreed that government regulation was the problem, but the solution to the problem was to impose *more* regulatory control over the industry. All the experts did agree, however, that there would be huge rate increases in our electric bills.

I am no expert on the electric power industry, and I have only a rudimentary understanding of why my light comes on when I flick a switch, so I am making no claim that I have an educated opinion on how to deal with the blackout problem. But had I been asked for my professional opinion during the early hours of the blackout, I would have had a completely different take on the situation. I would have raised only one question: What is the optimal blackout rate?

Almost every expert pointed out that after the last major blackout in 1977, the public was assured that after the subsequent improvements were made in the system, there would *never* be another major blackout. Well, that turned out not to be the case. Without missing a beat, almost every expert now argued that ultimately billions of dollars would have to be spent to update the system so that *this time* the problem would never happen again. Now as impressive as that claim is, I simply don't believe it. I doubt it is technically feasible to reduce the blackout rate completely to zero. And even if it is technically feasible, I have another question: *Is it worth it?*

There is no doubt that a massive blackout imposes substantial costs on society. Yet if billions are spent only to slightly reduce the blackout rate, the costs of reducing the rate may far exceed the *expected* benefits of reducing the rate. For example, assume a blackout imposes substantial social costs of $500 billion, and that an investment of only $25 billion can be spent to completely eliminate the blackout rate. This appears to be an excellent investment. But if the original blackout rate is 1%, and the new blackout rate is zero, that $25 billion investment doesn't save $500 billion but instead, *on average,* saves only 1% of $500 billion, or $5 billion. There simply may be no cost-effective way to completely eliminate the occasional blackout. And although it sounds very strange to argue that there is a positive optimal rate of power blackouts, it may very well be the case.

I believe the blackout issue provides an example of how a tragedy, in and of itself, may dictate public policy responses. As I discussed in chapter 2, it is important to detach yourself from the horror of a tragedy before considering appropriate policy solutions. I found it interesting that I didn't hear a single analyst conclude that maybe the best response would be to have no response at all. Just one major blackout in twenty-six years is pretty impressive. We may very well be able to get things back to normal and go another twenty-six years before another problem occurs. On the other hand, maybe there is a problem that needs to be fixed now, even at a substantial cost. What is the correct solution? Is there a *correct* solution?

THERE ARE ONLY TRADE-OFFS

I once heard an economist offer the following universal policy advice: *there are no solutions; there are only trade-offs.* My interpretation of that comment is that no matter what policy solution is offered for any particular social issue, that solution will never be satisfactory to everyone. There will always be trade-offs—costs and benefits—that make the concept of a "solution" ambiguous, at best. Even with an accurate measurement of the costs and benefits, you still have to deal with the problems of defining social welfare and identifying a policy objective.

I have a friend whose job puts him in a position to provide policy advice that could possibly have real-world impact. I once asked him how comfortable he was being in that position, and he had no qualms at all about it. He then asked me the following question: "If policy decisions have to be made, wouldn't you be happier having them made by economists rather than by anyone else?" That's a good question, and after thinking about it for a few minutes, I decided that no, I wouldn't be happier. If economists were making all the policy decisions, we would never be given credit when things turned out well, but we would quickly be blamed when things turned out badly. Who needs that kind of pressure? Not me, but I know plenty of economists who would enjoy nothing more than having their advice taken seriously. But exactly how good is economic policy advice? To address this question, I'd like to return to the issue of copyright protection and fair use (i.e., legal copying) I discussed in chapter 4.

How to resolve the classic trade-off between providing incentives to create intellectual property versus the problem associated with monopoly pricing has received a lot of attention from economists, especially recently. The Napster case caught the attention of several high profile, extremely well-respected economists. The merging of copying technology and the digital age brought the issue of fair use to the forefront of the debate on copyright protection in the music industry. As is often the case with a controversial social issue, some economists argued in favor of fair use for music file-sharing, and others warned of the dangers of financially crippling the music industry. This disagreement seems to lend credence to an old joke: if you put three economists together in one room, they will come out with four opinions. The debate over copyright protection provides an excellent setting to more closely examine exactly what it is economists agree and disagree about.

Economists generally agree on the fundamental *theoretical* trade-off that copyright protection presents: the ability to provide incentives for the creation of intellectual property versus the social loss of monopoly pricing. Also, they often agree on the definition of social welfare, as well as on the objective of social welfare maximization. But even with these agreements, they can disagree on the measurement, either formally or informally, of the appropriate costs and benefits. Some economists sincerely see music file-sharing as a threat to the future creation of intellectual property. Others believe that musicians can still thrive with no copyright protection. This type of disagreement may never easily be resolved, and it demonstrates just how difficult it is to apply opposing viewpoints to what eventually must be an actual policy decision.

In chapter 1 I discussed the difficulties of doing empirical work to measure trade-offs. To the extent that these difficulties lead to differences in the way economists measure costs and benefits, these differences do not depict a shortcoming in economic reasoning. Personally, I believe that when it comes to the type of social issues I discussed in this book, there are not many fundamental differences among most economists in the way they think about them. The differences that do exist often can be traced to the way economic reasoning typically must be quantified to make it applicable to real world issues.

Because of the difficulties involved in finding definitive policy solutions, many economists choose to adopt a consistent policy viewpoint across many issues. For example, some economists believe that markets almost always work, while others believe that markets rarely work. Some economists believe that if markets fail, they fail for reasons that cannot be alleviated by government intervention. Others believe that market failures *require* government intervention. Other economists, myself included, tend to take an issue by issue approach to public policy. I believe that markets have advantages and disadvantages relative to government intervention policies, and these trade-offs are often issue-specific. The bottom line is that opposing policy positions are unavoidable due to the open-ended nature of policy analysis. This holds true not only for economists, but for any public policy discipline.

AND IN MY OPINION

When I teach policy courses, I often get asked by my students to discuss my personal opinions about the social issues we study. There's never any reason for me to do this because my personal opinions have absolutely no bearing on what I want my students to learn in my courses. Furthermore, I'm not even sure I still have many personal opinions that can be distinguished from my professional opinions. I've been thinking about trade-offs for so many years that I rarely choose sides in an issue. Of course, if there is an issue that has a direct bearing on my life, I tend to have a personal opinion that may very well deviate from my professional opinion.

People tend to care about social issues in terms of how they are personally affected by policy proposals. This is only natural. Nonsmokers are likely to support antismoking laws; smokers are not. For example, the city of Athens, Ohio, where I live, was considering banning smoking in bars and restaurants. It was nice of the city to be considering that issue precisely when I was teaching about smoking in my health economics course. I asked my class how many of them supported the ban, and they were overwhelmingly in favor of it. I asked one specific student who raised her hand in support of the ban exactly why she supported it. She said that she was going to answer not based on any social consideration of the trade-offs, but only in terms of her personal feelings. She hated the smell of cigarette smoke. Period. Her answer impressed me as it demonstrated that she understood the difference between thinking about the issue in a social way versus a private way. On the final exam, however, she dealt with similar issues by only considering the social trade-offs. Smart student.

Instead of presenting my personal opinions about the social issues I've discussed in this book, I will summarize my approach to thinking about such issues. When considering personal risk-taking activities that *do not* adversely affect others, such as the individual decision to smoke, I find it difficult to justify social intervention to control such behavior. If individuals are making well-informed decisions, the usual paternalistic arguments in favor of social control are difficult for me to embrace. But if individuals are making poorly-informed decisions, or there is an added complication such as the possibility of addiction, the justification for social control is stronger. Still, precisely what form of social control to adopt is an extremely difficult question to answer. Should public policy provide information for individuals to make better-informed choices, or should there be direct control through banning or taxation?

The heart of the matter lies in whether or not individuals take actions that bother others. Private decisions can impose social costs on others. This is exactly what laws are designed to deal with. In dealing with these issues, I do have a bias. I believe that the place to start is with the possibility of a market solution. Can the issue of smoking in bars and restaurant be handled by market forces? Can product safety decisions be motivated by market forces? If yes, the costs of choosing and implementing social control policies may be avoided. Furthermore, market forces may have the ability to achieve the efficient outcome without anyone having to know exactly what that outcome is. This is a tremendous advantage of a free market.

A market solution, however, is neither necessary nor sufficient to achieve a socially efficient outcome. It is not necessary because there can be other ways to allocate resources, such as with organ conscription for transplants or with fair use to circumvent copyright protection. It is not sufficient because there may be market failures such as transactions costs or imperfect information that prevent the efficient allocation of resources from being achieved. A free market is a means to an end, not an end in and of itself.

It is obvious that using economic reasoning is not the only way to approach social issues, but I have met many economists who argue that it is the best way to think about them. Although I personally use economic reasoning when I think about social issues, I find it difficult to apply the word *best* to ways of thinking about the world. How one thinks about social issues is a subjective concept. I do believe, however, that economic reasoning is an important and valid way to think about public policy, and I hope that I have been able to convey that to you throughout this book. I try to teach my students to be comfortable with economic reasoning, but I do not teach them to accept it outside the scope of my course. That is something they have to make a personal decision to do. My hope is that even if they don't accept economic reasoning, they at least understand enough of it to appreciate why they don't accept it.

Actually, I tend to worry more about the students who embrace economic reasoning too quickly. When I taught at Texas A&M University in College Station, Texas, a fairly conservative town, I once gave a lecture about the trade-offs associated with legalizing prostitution and drugs. There was a student in my class who, at the time, was a student-teacher at a local middle school. He so enjoyed my lecture about the economics of sex and drugs that he decided to present it to his class of adolescents. That was his last day of student-teaching at that school! I guess I forgot to mention to him that as a teacher of controversial issues, it is important to know your audience.

DARE TO DREAM

Obviously, policy decisions must be made. What it is that policy officials actually care about is a wide open question. At one extreme, you can argue that policy officials are selfish and care only about their best interests. I know many economists who are very comfortable with this position. At the other extreme, you can argue that policy officials care only about the well-being of others. I don't know *any* economists who are comfortable with this position. My guess is that policy officials care about politics, and so they probably care a little bit about everything that one can imagine.

If I got to pick my version of a perfect policy world, I would like policy officials to explicitly recognize the concept of trade-offs. For example, concerning an issue such as banning smoking in bars and restaurants, I would applaud a politician who made the following statement:

> I have decided to support the ban of smoking in all public bars and restaurants. I feel that this will greatly benefit nonsmokers from being

bombarded with the deadly cigarette smoke of others. I recognize that smokers may be hurt by this policy by having their freedom to smoke curtailed. I also recognize that bar and restaurant owners may lose out if this policy reduces the profitability of their businesses. However, recognizing that there will be winners and losers to this policy, I sincerely believe that the benefits of this policy outweigh the costs.

Unfortunately, you would be much more likely to hear the following:

> I have decided to support the ban of smoking in all public bars and restaurants. I feel that this will greatly benefit nonsmokers from being bombarded with the deadly cigarette smoke of others. I also feel that this will benefit smokers who will now have fewer social opportunities in which to smoke, and this can only improve their health. This policy will also benefit bar and restaurant owners because their businesses will soar in profitably due to the large potential customer base of nonsmokers who will now, without hesitation, gladly patronize smoke-free establishments. I apologize if I have failed to recognize any other group of individuals who are also going to benefit from this policy.

I guess I can take solace in the fact that if the former statement was the more realistic of the two, it wouldn't have been as much fun to write this book.

NOTES

The quote "there are no solutions, there are only trade-offs" was made by Thomas Sowell at a talk he gave at Ohio University in 1992.

See the notes at the end of chapter 4 for references on the Napster case.

Index

automobile product design, 11

British Medical Journal, 83

Cherry, Don, 89–90
child poisoning, 90–91
cigarette addiction, 56–59
cigarette advertising, 59–61
competitive market, 35, 37
Consumer Product Safety Commission (CPSC), 90
contract law, 113–14
copyright protection, 36–43, 119–20
costs of production, 35
cotton dust, regulatory standards, 16–17
crime, economic analysis of, 5

death credit, smoking and, 79–82
defensive medicine, 95–98
demand, 34
design defect, 102–3
due care, 105–7

efficient theft, 26–28
electric power industry, 117–18
eminent domain, 30
empirical work, difficulties, 2–3
environmental tobacco smoke (ETS), 75–78, 82–84

fair use, 40–43, 119–20
Federal Aviation Administration (FAA), 16
Food and Drug Administration (FDA), 44
Ford Pinto, 10–11, 14, 17–19, 102–3
foreseeable misuse, 107–8
full price, 54–55, 109–11

gains from trade, 21–23, 70–72, 109–11

Handbook of Health Economics, 51
HIV, 91–93
Hockey Night in Canada, 89

incremental costs, 35, 40
insurance, 93–95
intellectual property, 36–40
invisible hand, 23

Jeepers Creepers 2, 33
just compensation, 30

liability rule, property right and, 73

manufacturing defect, 102–9
market failure, 23
market structure, 35
medical malpractice liability, 95–98
monopoly pricing, 35–38
Moore v. The Regents of the University of California, 23–25, 71

moral hazard, 93–95
movie piracy, 33–34

Napster, 39–40, 43, 119–120
negative externality, 67–68
negligence, 105–9
negotiation costs, 72–73
no liability, 109–11

Office of Technology Assessment, 95
organ conscription, 26–31, 41
organ transplants, 26–31
Occupational Safety and Health Administration (OSHA), 16
offsetting behavior, 88–93

patents, 43–47
pharmaceutical pricing, 43–47
physical externality, 68
policy objectives, 3–7
presumed consent, 29–30
private costs versus social costs, 17
product X, 49
product warnings, 111–12
profit maximization, 36
property right, well-defined, 72
property rule, property right and, 72
psychic externality, 68

rational addiction, 57–59
reinforcement effect, 57
Regulation, 50
risk perceptions, smoking and, 53–56

safety cap regulation, 90–91
scarcity, 15–16
Scherer, F. M., 46
seat belt laws, 88
smoking in public, 74–78
social tragedy, 17
social welfare maximization, 3–7
strict liability, 103–9
sunblock, 89
sunlight, property right over, 68–74
supply, 34–35

teenage smoking, 61–64
tort law, 101, 113–14
transactions costs, 23

up-front costs, 35

value of life estimate, 10–16

wage/risk trade-off, 12–14
warning defect, 112
wealth distribution, 5–6
wrongful death damages, 12